SELLING LEMONADE FOR FREE

D1732699

Chuck Wall, Ph.D.
Kimberly Walton

Kindness, Inc.
3704 Panorama Drive
Bakersfield, California 93306

The talented Laura Cordella Gates from Bakersfield, California, created the lemonade stand on the front cover and some of the graphics found throughout this book.

Publication of this book was made possible through a generous grant from the State Farm Insurance Companies. We deeply appreciate State Farm's commitment to encourage respect and dignity toward all people.

Kindness, Inc.
3704 Panorama Drive
Bakersfield, California 93306

ISBN 0-9654840-1-7
Printed in the United States of America

To my own Princess Di,
for her love, support and patience.
Chuck Wall

~ ~ ~ ~ ~

To my mother, Jeannette,
for her love and friendship;
to my husband, Richard,
for encouraging me through school;
to my children: Amy, April and Amber;
and to Chuck Wall,
for this wonderful opportunity.
Kimberly Walton

Acknowledgments

Selling Lemonade for Free has been a team effort. Not only did Kimberly and I work together very well, we had excellent support from a number of individuals who devoted many hours to making sure this book was accurate and consistent with our expectations.

Our editorial board consisted of Nancy Fieber, Kevin Handy, Corris Macon, Nancy Packard, Jan Rockoff and Mike Ryan. They were tough critics when it came to keeping or tossing stories we put before them.

We want to give special thanks to Nancy Packard for her outstanding editorial work on this book.

We also thank Gail Istre for her excellent work in editing and formatting of *Selling Lemonade For Free.*

Laura Gates contributed her imagination and obvious talent to create our front cover, and her 11-year-old sister Catarina Gates offered her version of the lemonade stand later in the book.

Our printers, Craiger Bolen and Shari Darke of Central Printing & Graphics in Bakersfield, California, along with their assistant Debbie Bowen spent many hours helping fine tune our book. We appreciate their efforts.

A book like this is only possible when contributors of stories and ideas about respect and dignity step forward to share their thoughts. You will meet them throughout this book. They are the people who ultimately make this book such a success. Thanks to each of you for your willingness to share.

Our families deserve a great deal of credit for putting up with the months of scattered papers and a numerous amount of hours with telephone work that passed between us refining ideas and stories.

We would love to thank all of our closest friends and family who listened to and helped put up with us during all the many months of preparation for this book. This is a difficult project and our support systems are one of our best assets. We hope that all of you will enjoy our final product.

~~*Chuck Wall and Kimberly Walton*

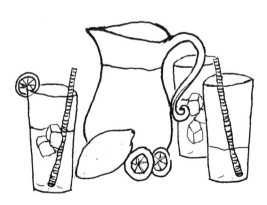

About Chuck Wall, Ph.D.

Chuck Wall is a published author, lecturer and motivational speaker in the fields of communications, stress management, employee motivation, leadership, and random acts of kindness.

After receiving an Associate of Arts degree from Bakersfield Community College, he earned a B.A. and an M.B.A. from San Francisco State University, followed by a Ph.D. in Educational Administration and Management from the University of California at Los Angeles. He has coauthored a book on organizational renewal, authored *The Kindness Collection* and *Teams: The Tenneco Way*. He produced and directed a multimedia look into the 21st century for the President of the United States and hosted his own television and radio programs. Dr. Wall has headed two of his own firms, one in publishing and the other in manufacturing.

Chuck is currently Professor of Communications and Human Relations at Bakersfield College. In 1992 he received the prestigious *Hayward Award* for teaching excellence in California community colleges. He is the past Chair of the Business and Education Committee of the Bakersfield Chamber of Commerce, President of the Kindness Foundation, and chaired the 1998 Kern County Governmental Charter Review Committee. At this time Dr. Wall is deeply involved in the Random Acts of Kindness movement which has received international attention. Last November he was the guest of the government of Singapore where he spoke about kindness as an international concept. His work with the creation of this movement has been recognized by the United States House of Representatives, which instituted an Act of Kindness Awareness Week for the United States. As a result of the kindness movement, Dr. Wall was the recipient of the Greater Bakersfield Chamber of Commerce Beautiful Bakersfield President's Award for 1994. He has appeared on some 250 television and radio programs in the United States, Canada, Singapore, and Australia, as well as special appearances on The Oprah Winfrey Show, The Hour of Power in 1994 and again in March, 2000, ABC Prime Time Live and CNN's Thanksgiving Day Special. He was the signature speaker for the International Million Dollar Roundtable Conference. In 1995 he was awarded the Hero of Peace Award for North America by Discovery Toys. In 1997 he received the Shirley Trembley Distinguished Teaching Award at Bakersfield College. Last year he was given the United Way/Bakersfield Centennial Foundation's From the Heart Award for Excellence in Education. A very proud moment came in 1997 when he took first place at the Kern County Fair for his redwood wild birdfeeders, which he makes in his home workshop.

Even though Chuck is blind, he does not consider himself disabled, but merely must spend extra time dealing with one of life's little nuisances.

About Kimberly Walton

Kimberly Walton conducts seminars and gives motivational speeches on looking good and feeling good. She writes articles for a local paper and various newsletters to motivate and encourage positive thinking and provides advice on cosmetics and personal appearance. She is a licensed cosmetologist who is living with Lupus (an autoimmune disease). She is currently attending Bakersfield College, working on a degree in Business Communications.

After meeting Dr. Wall she was moved to help him with his project of promoting kindness. Her experience with the many acts of kindness she has received from others was also her great motivator.

Kimberly realizes firsthand that most people have had to deal with overwhelming circumstances of life at one time or another. She feels that Dr. Wall is a great example of overcoming life's difficulties and is happy to be a part of this great project.

Kimberly currently resides in Bakersfield, California, with her husband, Richard, and daughters, April and Amber. Her oldest daughter, Amy, lives in Los Angeles, California.

Simply give others, a bit of yourself,

a thoughtful act, a helpful idea,

a word of appreciation,

a lift over a rough spot,

a sense of understanding.

a timely suggestion.

You take something out of your mind,

garnished in kindness out of your heart,

and put it into the other fellow's mind and heart.

~~Charles H. Burr

This Book Was Written...

...to thank all of the people who commit their many acts of kindness. We thank you and commend you for all the wonderful kind things you continue to commit in your life. These acts of kindness do not go unnoticed. Without you in this world we would be in a terrible situation. Each and every time you open a door or help someone feel good about him- or herself we thank you. Each time you see the kindness phrase "Today, I will commit one random act of senseless KINDNESS... Will You?" we are thanking you. Take this thank you into your heart and continue to commit your acts of kindness. Every word you read in this book is a "thank you" to you!

As you read the stories in this book, we want you to think about how they might help you create the kindness you want in your own life. Remember that kindness is made up of equal parts of respect, dignity, compassion and humility.

~~Chuck Wall, Ph.D.
~~Kimberly Walton

Whoever in trouble and sorrow

needs your help,

give it to him.

Whoever in anxiety or fear

needs your friendship,

give it to him.

It isn't important whether he likes you.

It isn't important whether

you approve of his conduct.

It isn't improtant what

his creed or nationality may be.

~~E. N. West

The Kindness Story

Alternately I have been blessed and con-demned for creating the sentence, "Commit a random act of kindness." Here is the truth – *I DID NOT* create this phrase, but I may well be responsible for what is now a worldwide movement! There are references to random acts of kindness in literature going back centuries. I am going to tell you how it happened for me because it has changed my life...for the better, I might add.

It began in early September 1993. I was having breakfast and listening to the news on the radio. I never just listen to the radio; I am always off thinking about something else. My mind seems to work like the first line of a poem I once heard: "Each thing I do, I rush through, so I can do something else." So while listening to the news, I was also thinking about something different to engage the minds of my Human Relations and Motivation students at Bakersfield College. What could I do that I hadn't done already?

Since the news is rarely uplifting, I was only vaguely aware of the newscaster's comments until he dramatically proclaimed, "Ladies and gentlemen, today we have another random act of senseless violence to report." My immediate reaction was one of anger. *VIOLENCE, VIOLENCE!* Is that all we can talk about these days? Isn't there anything else that can hold our attention besides another random act of senseless violence?

As I began to calm down, I started the process of

word association. What is in that phrase that I might use to launch an assignment for my students? What if I took out *violence* and inserted *kindness*? What I had then was, "Ladies and gentlemen, today we have another random act of senseless *kindness* to report."

I walked into my 9 a.m. Human Relations class, instructed the students to take out paper and pen, and to write down the following: "Today, I will go out into the community and commit one random act of senseless...," and at this point I waited for them to catch up..."*kindness*." I got the usual questions. Is this going to count toward our grades, and how much is it worth? Does the paper have to be typed? What's a kindness? Give us your definition.

I answered all questions except the last. I didn't want them to write about what they thought *I* believed to be kindness but rather what *they* thought kindness meant. "This assignment is due in two weeks. Happy hunting!" I said. Had I been more specific, the students would not have shown the variety of ideas they were capable of generating.

Here are just a few glimpses of their efforts. You will read about some of them in greater detail in this collection. One woman took her daughter to visit patients in a convalescent hospital, one gave up her parking space in a full lot, and another found a stray collie and, with creative effort, located the owner. A young man paid his mother's electric bill with money he earned during the summer, and two students took furry, stuffed animals to the children's ward of a local hospital.

While this was meant to be just an assignment

to be turned in for a grade, that's not the way it worked. One of the students, Jo Marshall, without my knowledge, contacted a reporter from the local newspaper, *The Bakersfield Californian* . Jo thought this might make a good story. The reporter, Liz Barker, went to her editor, told him about it, and asked if he thought it was worth covering. He left it up to her. Rather than come to my office in person, Liz called a very surprised me and conducted a less than enthusiastic interview by telephone.

After she had time to think about it, the assignment I had given didn't seem so kooky after all. In fact, the article ran on the front page of the Saturday edition. The class and I were pleased with the newspaper's coverage of a *good* news story and enjoyed the attention we received for a few days. Within a week we were on to the next assignment and all was forgotten except the newspaper clipping.

Then I received another telephone call. This time it was from Nancy Mayer, a reporter for *The Associated Press* . She came across the kindness article while perusing newspaper stories from Central California. She asked if she could come to Bakersfield for a day to interview me and get the reactions regarding this assignment from my students. At the end of the following week Nancy had her story, but she warned me not to get my hopes up. Frequently stories just seem to die somewhere in the system.

Nearly three weeks had gone by and the interview was becoming a dim memory. Then on Friday of the third week Nancy called. "You may want to get ready. The editors in New York have decided to run the story on the wire and send it to every radio and television station and every newspaper they are associated with around the world! You might get a phone call or two." The next week the story ran in about 1,000 newspapers, on television news shows and radio programs.

We didn't get a few phone calls—we got thousands! We lost track of the calls when the switchboard at Bakersfield College was jammed for several days. Interview requests poured in and I found myself doing five or six radio programs per day, often starting at 5:00 a.m. and doing all night shows on the East Coast. Charles Osgood of CBS radio did an *Osgood File* report. Then the mail started arriving. First by 10 or 20, then by the hundreds of letters each day for months on end!

The Crusaders television program spent a week with us in November 1993. The audience response was so great from this episode that a follow-up segment was immediately planned. It involved me talking with a group of teenagers who had recently experienced a random act of senseless violence. Some of their parents were aboard the Long Island commuter train in which a gunman randomly opened fire. I began by asking them to tell me about themselves—where they live, about their parents, brothers and sisters, their high school activities, their hopes and dreams for the future. Together we began to plan community activities in which they could become involved. The objective was to see if by becoming involved in others' lives, they might turn their pain and anger regarding this act of violence away from their need for vengeance and toward the realization that their energies might be used positively in other areas.

Another shift in our lives came from that trip to New York. A United States Congressman, Walter Tucker (D-California), contacted *The Crusaders* to say he wanted to introduce a congressional resolution to the House of Representatives, declaring one week each year as "Kindness Awareness Week." *The Crusaders* staff put his legislative assistant in touch with me and we began developing the wording for the resolution. When asked what week I thought would be best for this national celebration, I suggested the week of Feb. 14. The week was accepted, presented to Congress, and received a unanimous *"YES"* vote on the floor of the House of Representatives. At the conclusion of this collection you will find a copy of the original resolution Congressman Tucker circulated among his colleagues.

At the same time the State Caucus Chair from Pennsylvania contacted me to collaborate on the wording of a Pennsylvania state resolution. This was the first of many states to declare kindness awareness days and weeks.

CNN came to my classroom and aired a story that went around the world. Now calls were coming from Russia, England, France, Sweden, Germany, Canada, and Puerto Rico. But the most memorable came from Doris Bacon, a reporter for *People* magazine. She scheduled a day to spend with my class and discover what all the fuss was about. Her article was published in the Dec. 13, 1993, issue. I remember this clearly because on the front cover of the magazine was a picture of Lorena Bobbitt and her knife. Actually, my story followed hers, and, as my wife, Di, pointed out, it was better to be *after* Mrs. Bobbitt than for Mrs. Bobbitt to be *after* me!

Appearances on *The Oprah Winfrey Show* in February 1994, and as a guest of Dr. Robert Schuller at the Crystal Cathedral during his *Hour of Power* brought the message of kindness to people in 100 countries. The challenge to commit a random act of kindness has touched millions of people in the United States. Those who work hard to improve their communities are often lost in the dust of those getting attention by destroying our American way of life. Is it the fault of our government, our church, and our schools? No, it is your fault and mine for *allowing* this to happen. We *can* solve the problem, and it really isn't that difficult. Just begin the process in your own home, school, church, and community. Treat others the way you want to be treated. Respect and dignity guide each of us to a solution for our nation's violence. Will this solve all of our problems? Not at all, but respect and dignity will go a long way to divert attention *away* from violence and *toward* kindness.

When we began our kindness assignment, my students suggested I create something that would help people remember what they were trying to do. They suggested a bumper sticker, which is now seen around the world and has been printed on more than 250,000 stickers. The kindness phrase also appears on T-shirts, posters and magnets.

In my book, *The Kindness Collection*, ordinary people not seeking recognition told how they worked to improve their own lives as well as those around them. As you read, you may find the inspiration to do something positive for others around you. I challenge each of you: "Today, I will commit one random act of senseless KINDNESS...*Will You?"*

Since 1996 when *The Kindness Collection* was published, much has occurred to encourage kindness over violence. I have given several hundred speeches about acts of kindness throughout the United States to audiences that are truly interested in improving their own lives and their community environment. *The Kindness Collection* was very quickly a complete sell out. Thanks to the generosity of State Farm Insurance Companies, this new book *Selling Lemonade For Free* is now a reality. In 1999, when speaking at a conference on acts of kindness in Singapore, I learned just how extensively the concept has traveled around the world. Many nations, including Japan, Australia, Thailand, Korea, and Canada, as well as Singapore, have made kindness the centerpiece of national efforts to curb violence and encourage respect and dignity among all people.

Today schools both public and private, and at all levels, have adopted kindness as a way of encouraging students and staff alike to participate in kindness rather than violence. In addition, many businesses have participated by developing creative kindness programs to reduce stress and frustration from our fast-paced way of life.

Our two web sites, *www.kindnessinc.org* and

www.kindnessusa.org, continue to receive many visitors who are interested in learning how they can become a part of this worldwide movement. There is now a world kindness day, November 13, and here in the United States we celebrate kindness awareness each year during the week of February 14. It is the hope of both Kimberly and me that, when the next book is ready for publication, every country on the planet will have some type of kindness program in place. We have to continue our optimistic outlook—it's what keeps all of us looking forward to tomorrow.

~~Chuck Wall, Ph.D.
President, Kindness, Inc.

I expect to pass through this life but once.
If, therefore, there be any kindness I can show,
or any good thing I can do for any fellow being,
let me do it now... as I shall not pass this way again.

~~William Penn

A Compassionate Horse?

Cody is my twenty-nine-month-old quarter horse. He loves other horses, people and most of all, his friend, my dog, Arizona. When I first purchased Cody, he had little contact with humans or animals other than those at his breeder's ranch. The first time he saw another rider on a horse sent him running. His first introduction to Arizona was a lick fest. He let Arizona lick his nose while they got familiar with another, which is now a ritual they go through each time they come in contact. He has expanded this ritual to include a full-face licking! Cody isn't a unique horse in liking "his" dog, but having a horse that likes other critters is a big plus for how they relate to humans.

He is now learning to carry a rider. We were on a trail with my partner and his horse who were serving as role models for Cody. Cody and I were riding up a graded slope from the river to the main trail, and younger inexperienced horses have a tendency to leap. They aren't sure of their footing (or how to use their muscles properly) on slopes. I was taking things very slowly since working with a young horse is a new experience for me. As we reached level ground, he kept his head down in the slope-climbing position and suddenly began to buck. After the third buck, I bailed off, landing flat on the ground. I got the wind knocked out of me, was speechless, banged and bruised, but was not seriously injured. Cody ran ahead, but after realizing something was missing from his back, he turned around with a Little puzzled look at his now-empty saddle. He looked further and found me on the ground. His expression seemed to say—what happened to you?

This 1,200-pound horse immediately came right back to me placing his muzzle into the crook of my neck and calmly reassuring me that everything was going to be okay. You get a true sense of how large a horse is when you are on the ground looking up at one of them. As I lay there, I was surprised to think that I had no fear of him stepping on me or running away. It was as if he were a compassionate, guardian angel.

Cody gently nuzzled my neck as he watched me with his sensitive, big brown eyes, and he was as gentle as a kitten could have been. His nose did not break contact with me until my partner was able to help me up off the ground.

My partner insisted I get back on him to make the trek back to the barn. Although I was sore and shaken, I was glad I did. I felt a closeness to Cody that was indescribable. We already had a trusting bond, but now whenever I think of him or see him, my heart fills with love stemming from his kindness.

~~*Joan Finnegan*

A Wave

How do you feel when someone waves to you? It's a good feeling, isn't it? So "hand" a few out yourself. You can wave in a friendly way that says "hello" or "thank you" to anyone.

Little American Tourist

Afew years ago my mom, little sister and I took a trip to Europe. When we arrived in London, we were tired and hungry. Needless to say, we were all eager to find our hotel. My mom decided that the "tube" (or subway) could get us there quickly and directly without much hassle. Unfortunately, about half way through our pleasant little journey, we found out that some work was being done on the tracks ahead and the passengers would have to get off the train soon. We stayed on until the last possible stop, then grudgingly gathered up our massive suitcases and began to push our way through the crowd to the street. About half way up my arms were straining so much that I couldn't carry my luggage one step further. Oblivious that I had stopped, my mom and sister kept walking, and I was quickly losing sight of them. I began to get frustrated, not knowing what to do. Suddenly, out of the crowd, a man came up to me. He didn't say much—just picked up all of my luggage and said, "Come on." This man not only carried my things to the street, but he walked me to the bus stop with my family and even helped us safely onto the bus. I thanked him repeatedly, but I don't think he realized just how appreciative I was. Naturally, I never saw that man again, but I haven't forgotten him either. With hundreds of people around, he was the only one who chose to stop and help an exhausted little American tourist, and for that I will always be grateful.

~~Laura Gates

What Is A Pass-along Thank You?

This is an idea I had many years ago when I wanted to sincerely thank the people who helped me in a time of need. I could not remember the names of those who helped me but their kindness is never forgotten. I thought about putting it in the paper, but what was the chance they would see the story? And how would they know I was thanking them without knowing their names? So, after getting involved with Dr. Wall in writing this book, I thought what a wonderful way for others, as well as myself, to thank those who either like to remain anonymous or whose names we can't remember! We need to remember the positive things—the "good news" as Dr. Wall would say—by remembering the good things that happen in life. So let's get started. Here is how it works.

We all know how quickly the grapevine method of communication passes along some interesting story amongst friends. Well, this is the way for the grapevine method to be used in a positive way to thank people for acts of kindness. This book has included stories that are true and were written in the hopes that people like you will spread the word-of-mouth grapevine which will eventually reach the recipients that the stories were written about and were worthy of being passed along. Just like when you see a great movie, you talk about it to your friends, don't you? That is what we want you to do with this book. Pass these stories along; tell them to your friends so the people who committed the acts of kindness can be thanked, and so others can see examples of how to commit their own acts of kindness. So everywhere you see the illustrated grapevine in this book, you have found a pass-along thank you. Read it and tell your friends about it!

Now for the most exciting part! We want you to contact our web site and tell us if you think that any of these stories were written about you. We also want you to "tell on others" who commit acts of kindness. You might call it a "tell-a-kindness site," or send your own pass-along thank you to our kindness website at 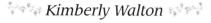 _www.kindnessinc.org_. Let us know what you think of the book. Have fun with this—we can't wait to hear from you!

Kimberly Walton

Kindness Strikes Twice
A Pass-along Thank You

While driving home from work one afternoon in the summer of 1982, my car ran out of gas. Even though I could see the gas station ahead of me, a man and his wife insisted that they help me out. This was a humbling experience for me that normally didn't occur. But I was recently separated from an abusive husband and was very low on money and fuel as well.

About two months after this incident, my husband was arrested for threatening my life. Late that night a concerned police officer told me if I had some place safe to go, I should get there before he was released sometime early the next day.

Desperate for refuge from future abuse, I felt forced to flee immediately for the safety of my children's lives and my own. It was only a number of hours before he would be released. Throughout the night I packed only the necessities into the trunk of the car as quickly and efficiently as possible.

First thing the next morning I sold all of our furniture to a used furniture store in town. I had decided to drive to California where my parents lived so my husband couldn't locate me.

I was tired and scared, and in the last moments of desperation before leaving town, I remembered a trucking company nearby. Maybe someone there could share some helpful road advice with me, or, better yet, have a truck driver that I could follow to California.

I asked the person at the front desk of Bekins Van Lines if any of the drivers were going to California or even some place close. I had grown up in this small town in Kansas, and I had no previous road experience. I knew it was a long, dangerous and difficult trip to make by myself with two small children. The Bekins clerk informed me there was one man driving to California (if he had not left town already), and that I was welcome to wait and see if he showed up. I decided it was worth the wait. I was in no position to attempt a drive of such distance without some advice for the rules of the road.

After a seemingly short wait the man arrived. I cautiously approached him and explained my idea about following his truck to California, but I didn't want to be a burden to him or interfere with his trip in any way. I suddenly realized it was the same man and his wife who had helped me when I ran out of gas weeks earlier. What a coincidence! Or was it?

With no hesitation the man said that I could follow him. The man, his wife, and their young son were going to visit a daughter that was living in Lancaster, California, and only one hour from where I was going. Not only did the couple see to it that my two children and I made the three-day trip together safely, but the kind couple even paid for a few of our meals and his wife helped me drive when I was too exhausted to do so. The man carefully checked the oil and water in my car when we stopped for gas, and their son even played with my children in the back seat of my car to keep them entertained. These were some extraordinary people!

Even though I thanked them then, I was in no state of mind to show them how truly thankful I was for their help. I hope somehow they will hear this story and know how much I appreciated all the kindness they administered to my small children and me in the few days that our lives connected. Please tell this story to someone who will pass it along. Maybe it will reach the kind people who touched me with kindness not once, but twice.

Kimberly Walton

Movie Seats

One evening my husband and I went to see a movie. Just before the movie began an elderly couple entered the theater looking for seats together. Of course since the movie was popular and almost ready to begin, there were only a few seats available, all of which were on opposite ends of a row or nowhere near each other. My husband and I glanced through the theater and then asked a row of people if they would kindly move down a seat, leaving two free seats on the end of the row for the elderly couple to sit together. We never think that something so simple could make such a difference, but it does!

~~Gretchen Penner

Happy Birthday Balloon

I am a residential apartment manager and I usually manage buildings for the elderly. I have found that many of them have no friends or family and may not even remember how old they are. Some of them have even forgotten their own birthday. So every day I blow up a simple balloon and write Happy Birthday with the name of the birthday person on it and tie it to the door of the apartment before he or she wakes up.

You can't imagine how excited they get over something so simple. I tried buying the balloons with "Happy Birthday" already printed on them, but the birthday person would bring the balloon back to me and ask me to reprint Happy Birthday in my own handwriting. It became more of a personal message if I took the time to write on the balloon myself. People always feel special to know someone cares about and remembers them.

One woman came downstairs from her apartment proudly showing her balloon and asking me how old she was today. She showed it to everyone she saw, from the mailman to the people standing in the corridors who were there to visit someone else. As she happily proclaimed she was 92 years old, I felt the gratification that I had hoped for.

~~Jeannette Osborn

Don't Take My Joy

Is it hard for you to accept a kindness from someone? It is uncomfortable for some people even to accept a compliment, so you can imagine how difficult it is for people to accept someone doing something kind for them. One of the best pieces of advice I have ever received was from an elderly friend of mine who was trying to do something nice for my children and me.

As I repeatedly refused to let her buy us dinner because she lives on a small income, she said, "Don't take my joy. I want to do this and it is the only thing I can do to feel I have helped or done something kind for someone. Please allow me to do this!" Well, I certainly saw her point. So I swallowed my pride and said, "Thank you very much; what a kind thing for you to do." I truly allowed myself to enjoy the moment for her sake instead of feeling bad or guilty. She was so happy to have been able to do what she intended to do—something kind. Now I use this same phrase if someone refuses my help. Try it!

~~*Kimberly Walton*

*If you have not often felt joy of doing a kind act,
You have neglected much, and most of all yourself.*
~~*A. Neilen*

Here's Your Bill

The act of kindness that I have committed comes with a price. This price is difficult for some to pay, but it is customary where an act of kindness is concerned. I hope not to inconvenience you too much, but this is all I ask of you.

The price that I want is for you to allow me to commit my act of kindness free of charge. If you allow me to present this act of kindness to you, then I will receive the joy I would like to receive for committing it.

Your portion of the bill is paid in full when you truly enjoy the act itself, without feeling as though you owe me something in return. The fulfillment I get from this is all I want. So consider your bill paid in full!

~ ~ ~ ~

ATTENTION READERS:

This bill was designed to aid you in your kindness adventures! Please feel free to copy it and issue it to anyone who will not accept your act of kindness readily.

We have provided a *Kindness Bill* on the back page for your convenience.

The Language Of Kindness

What is the language of kindness? In the words of Mark Twain, "Kindness is the language the blind can see and the deaf can hear." People are all different, of course, but no one is perfect; we all have something about us that someone somewhere would term imperfect or flawed. Some of the flaws may be limitations that are with us for life, while others invade our lives for short periods of time, but are no less intense. Some people have physical limitations and some have mental limitations—some we can see and others we cannot see. There are cultural differences and racial differences, and no one has been successful in bringing all groups together happily. We are going to give suggestions in this book that can help bridge some of the gaps between the many cultural, ethnic, physical, mental, and socio-economical differences among the population today. In this section you will see that kindness and tolerance go hand in hand—a little patience and incentive to try something new and different and to sometimes be in unfamiliar circumstances—welcoming someone different than us, no matter what the difference, into our world, or us into theirs.

In this book you will find something written to encourage you to tread into unfamiliar territory, even if only for a moment. Take enough time to acknowledge someone's presence and/or carry on a conversation with someone you feel is different than you—someone you may feel you would not have attempted to get to know because of the differences between you.

How can this transpire? By the willingness to attempt it. The hearing can communicate with the deaf, the deaf with the hearing. The mentally challenged and the physically challenged can converse and interact with those who are not seemingly challenged. The young can help the mature, or the mature can help the young. This area of the book holds examples of how you can start that connection process.

Look for the glass and pitcher of lemonade or anything titled "The Language of Kindness" and you will find one of these suggestions. This section has been written by people who are experts because they have dealt or are dealing with one of these differences, or because they have been trained in a specific field of human diversity. Helping us learn to accept differences is a wonderful way to connect to many different types and kinds of people in this world.

Look For This Picture

Two Cousins
The Language of Kindness

F or years I've worked in the nonprofit world and vowed to myself I would only work for an agency or foundation that I have a heart-felt conviction for and which is concerned with individual differences. I now work for Bakersfield ARC, known locally as BARC (Bakersfield Association for Retarded Citizens).

This agency is a service provider and advocacy organization on behalf of citizens with developmental disabilities. As the Assistant Director of Community Affairs, I have the duty to educate and inform the community about BARC. I also have the privilege of touring guests around the facility and explaining the program's offerings. I love my job here and look forward to giving the tours. It's important for me to remember most people aren't comfortable around people who are developmentally disabled. To help the visitor get over that uneasiness, I will frequently stop and have a short conversation with or say hello to someone who is living with one of these disabilities.

By doing this, I've noticed two things. The visitors become more relaxed after spending time talking with someone who is a little different than they are, and the person living with the disability is happy to meet someone new who took time to talk with him.

People who are developmentally disabled will accept anyone they are meeting for the first time, without making a judgment. It would be wonderful if all people reacted that way. However, if you have a negative reaction to him, then he will react with hesitation. Usually someone with a developmental disability has tremendous insight to uncomfortable feelings. This must be a God-given protection that is never outgrown.

I myself have never had an uncomfortable feeling around someone who was different than I was because of my upbringing. I grew up with two cousins who are developmentally disabled. Coincidentally both are named Danny, but they are from different sides of the family. They didn't seem strange to me as a child, just different. I don't remember learning to become comfortable around them. Growing up as I did, accepting these differences and working around my cousins helped me naturally be accepting of all people, and their differences, with or without a disability.

A person with a disability is the same as any other person, just someone with a smile or a story to tell. I grew up with these two cousins just as I grew up with the others. I believe if more people had that opportunity they may not have such an uncomfortable feeling around someone different than they are.

One Danny has cerebral palsy, and his eyes go in different directions as you talk to him, his speech is distorted and hard to understand, and his body movements are erratic. The other Danny's physical movements aren't as erratic, but his child-like voice doesn't match his physical appearance. Yet, when this Danny grew older, he learned to live independently, work, and pay his own bills. When we were young and would play with either Danny, we were more patient and understanding, explaining things to him so that he could participate. And if he didn't understand the circumstances, then we praised him as if he did.

I remember an incident that made me feel bad for a long time. It happened when my best friend came over to my house on a day when one of the two Dannys was visiting. My friend made fun of the fact that I had a mentally retarded cousin and I joined her in making fun of him. Like other fifth graders might do, we sat and giggled and called him names. Luckily he didn't know what was being said and he laughed with us, making us laugh even more. I felt immense guilt come over me when I felt his innocence coming through, and I changed my attitude towards this immaturity and vowed never to do it again. Then I worked to reestablish a sense of pride in my cousin and myself.

My two cousins have been in my life for forty-some years now and I'm grateful because I've learned to look at a disability as...well, I don't know that I look at a disability at all. I just see a person, and I hope you will too.

~~Jan Callagy

A Heart For A Hart
A Pass-along Thank You

My name is Bonnie Hart and I am the appreciative recipient of a heart transplant. I had been experiencing heart problems for about five years, and although I wanted to live in denial about how serious my condition was, my doctor began running tests on me to see if I was a good candidate for a heart transplant. In December 1999 I was put on a waiting list for a heart. The waiting lists are very long, and many people die before they can receive the needed transplant because their bodies can no longer function.

Once you qualify for the transplant and your name is put on the list, you receive a pager. This is vital because the hospital must contact you immediately in the event an organ becomes available, and you will have two hours in which to get to the hospital to be prepped for surgery. If you can't be reached at home by phone, the pager keeps you from missing that call. Of course, this happens only if people are willing to donate their loved one's organs so that someone else may benefit.

My phone rang at 3:20 a.m. on April 12, 2000, and I was told that the hospital had a heart for me. This is an extremely emotional experience because this phone call would represent an opportunity at a new life or an immediate death in a matter of hours.

The donor of my new heart was a young, healthy individual who had been in an accident and was now left on life support. I can't begin to tell you all the things that went through my mind. I was thankful that a donor was found in time, and yet very upset that someone died so that I could live. One family grieving and one family rejoicing. I find it very difficult to discuss without crying.

I would like to thank the family of the donor! Because this kind family was willing to let their loved one's life be passed on to others, I now have a healthy heart. This family donated what organs they could from their loved one so that others could also benefit. I can't begin to express the gratitude that my family and I hold for the donor's family.

However, my sons have summed it up quite well. On Mother's Day of this year my youngest son, Todd, sent me a card thanking me for being a good mother as well as thanking the donor's mother for her kindness which allows me to live. He wrote, "We all thank God for your second chance and I hope on this Mother's Day that the mother of your heart's donor knows that she did the best thing that she could have done for her child—knowing her child's death saved someone, and that someone is you! I hope this is the first of many more Mother's Days."

My oldest son, Mark, now sends all of his email and any letters or correspondence with this saying, "My mother is alive today because someone was kind enough to be an organ donor. Have a "heart" and "donate" it. The life it saves may be closer to yours than you think."

Our lives were touched tremendously by some-one else's kindness. The hugs and kisses I share to-day are because of that kindness. As is customary with organ transplant survivors, I was given a new birthday on April 12th, 2000.

Please share this story with others and sign your donor cards today! This is one of the kindest things you could ever do for someone. Just think of the kind-ness that you will be passing on when you "pass on."

Bonnie Hart

When you donate an organ, you extend a life!

A Smile

Asmile leaves a lasting impression and some people are even known for their won-derful, pleasing smiles. They come in every shape and size and can become contagious as soon as they are seen. You can even hear a smile in someone's voice when you are talking to him or her on the phone. We can feel better about ourselves immedi-ately if we put a smile on our face.

A smile is free—you can give one away or you can receive one. If you give it away, be ready to get one back. And if you don't get one back immediately, then hang on to the one you have so you can give it to the next person that comes along.

Kindness Is...

An act that positively influences the life of both the giver and the receiver is a kindness. It doesn't have to cost money or be difficult to perform. It can be spontaneous (random) or premeditated. It can be as simple as a smile or a thank you, or as complicated as starting a nonprofit organization to benefit those in need.

Kindness has four working parts: dignity, respect, compassion and humility. If you have all of these things for yourself, then you will be able to share them with others. If we reach out with dignity, respect, compassion and humility, we are likely to feel it being returned.

Actively seeking out opportunities to assist others will naturally bring a certain amount of warmth and feeling of self-worth to each of us. It feels good to help others and others feel good knowing someone wants to help them.

"Consideration" and "helpful" are words often used to describe a kind deed. Kindness is what you define it as, rather than what someone else thinks you should believe it is.

I suggest all people actively attempt to live by my phrase: "Today, I will commit one random act of senseless KINDNESS. Will you?"

~~Chuck Wall, Ph.D.

A Word From A Teacher

One very memorable "act of kindness" happened to me when I was sitting next to some parents during a graduation ceremony. Because I am a faculty member, I was dressed in the normal graduation attire. One of the parents and I had been chatting for awhile when she turned to me and said, "Thank you for being a teacher!" I was thrilled, complimented, and very pleased. I will never forget this woman's brief, heartwarming comment!

As a teacher, I work very hard to provide my students with a positive learning environment. One of the highest compliments that I receive as a teacher is when students ask questions, no matter how silly they seem to be. I know then that I have created an atmosphere of trust. I feel acknowledged, validated, and privileged to be a teacher when students simply "ask."

On a final note, a simple "thank you" from my students can be the best pick-me-up! So if there are teachers that have touched your life, take a moment to share your appreciation with them. Your kindness will always be remembered.

~~Jeri Haner

Good Samaritans
A Pass-along Thank You

I t was about five o'clock in the evening on a Sunday afternoon in July of 1997. My wife, Star, and I were rolling along very smoothly in our 27-foot Class A motor home. Suddenly a lady passing by us began honking and waving and pointing to the rear of the motor home.

Looking back through the rear window, I saw smoke that was undoubtedly coming from our vehicle. I immediately started pulling over to try to stop. This took longer than expected since we were driving 60 miles per hour and towing a car. Once I stopped, I ran to the rear of the motor home. I thought one of the tires on the tow dolly had gone flat and caught fire.

However, this was not the case. To my horror, I noticed the flames under the motor home extended from the engine back to the rear axle. My immediate concern was getting my wife out of the "co-pilot's" seat since she is unable to walk. I was fearful that between the gas in the car in tow and the propane tank on the motor home there could be an explosion at any moment. As I hurried to get Star out of the vehicle, a man driving in the opposite direction stopped his car and ran across four lanes of traffic to help me. I gave him one of the two fire extinguishers as I pushed Star's wheel chair out of danger. Then I returned to help fight the fire.

By this time a second young man also came running across four lanes of speeding freeway traffic to help us. Both of these fellows put their lives in danger just trying to cross the freeway, and then, in spite of the smoke and fiery flames, both men crawled on their backs under the coach and put out the fire.

We determined that the transmission had sprung a leak and the oil dropping on a hot exhaust pipe had caught fire. Even though a very expensive repair job was ahead of us, we were ever so thankful and appreciative for the help of those two "Good Samaritans." Not only did they save our motor home, they probably saved our lives.

Please pass along our thanks and appreciation to those men. Only one of the men left his name—Thomas Hinkle from Meadow Vista, California. If this story is passed by word of mouth to enough people, hopefully this thank you will reach the other rescuer as well.

 Eddy Royeton

In the time we have it is surely our duty
to do all the good we can
to all the people we can
in all the ways we can
                                    ~~William Barclay

The Honeymoon Thank You

My husband and I were leaving San Juan, Puerto Rico, and heading home to California. While we were waiting for our flight to leave, we decided to browse through the gift shops. As we entered the perfume and jewelry shop, I spotted a coin purse on the floor. I opened it up to find a driver's license, credit cards, and a house key. I looked around the shop to see if I might recognize someone from the driver's license. But gee, would you want anyone to recognize you from your driver's license?

Not finding anyone matching the picture, I continued looking for someone who might be frantically looking for the lost coin purse. I spotted no one. I thought about turning the coin purse into the lost and found, but my husband warned against it. If it reached the hands of someone dishonest, that person might fraudulently put charges on the cards. I decided to mail it to the address on the driver's license when we returned home to California.

Several weeks later I received an appreciative thank-you letter from the owner of the coin purse. She said she had lost the purse as she was departing for her honeymoon in the Caribbean. She was so thankful that someone was honest enough to return it, and that someone would take the time to make sure the item was returned to the proper owner. I was glad she took time out of her busy schedule to let me know she received the purse, and it made me happy that she appreciated my efforts.

~~Victor and Pattie Mungary

Terra At The End Of The Bed
The Language of Kindness

On occasion because of my illness I have had to spend many days, weeks, or months in bed. I was only in my thirties, but being ill made me feel older than I was. Normally I held down a full-time job and raised three young children alone. My unexpected illness wreaked havoc on our lives because of the financial and emotional strain it brought to our household. It is frustrating when you can't take care of yourself—let alone your children. You lose touch with friends and feel unconnected to the rest of the world. Sometimes I was even too sick to watch television or read. People are busy with their own lives and it seems they forget about you.

Once in a while I received an unexpected knock at the door and to my surprise my children would inform me it was one of the young teenagers from our church. She would say that she was thinking of me and wondered if it was all right if she came in to visit. Explaining that I was very ill (which she knew but not how ill), I told her I would love for her to visit, but I wasn't well enough to sit up on the couch. If she really wanted to, she was welcome to sit at the end of the bed to talk with me. Without batting an eye, Terra said, "I will sit at the end of your bed then."

And she did. Terra would tell me all of the latest things I was missing out on at church, and the funny and not-so-funny things going on in her own life. Words cannot describe how much I appreciated this teenager's time and interest in me during my illness. It was such a special thing for her to visit with me rather than spend time with healthy friends her own age. She certainly touched my heart. Because of Terra's compassion, I at least felt somewhat connected to the outside world. Even today I look back on those not-so-happy days and remember the bright spots that Terra brought to my day, sitting at the end of my bed.

~~Kimberly Walton

Instant Gratification

We expect instant gratification in this world today and we are not patient enough to wait for the little things in life to happen. We rush, rush, rush and expect everyone else to do the same. Take a little time to slow things down a bit today. See if your day goes a little smoother. Take some time to help someone or do something for someone else today.

Willingness of a Child

Have you ever noticed the willingness of a small child to help someone out in a time of need? I remember my older daughter always offering a helping hand to my younger daughter when she needed help climbing up a hill. Children love to help change the baby or carry something into the house. Doing something to help someone makes him or her feel important.

My children used to come home from school and ask if they could take some of their belongings to school for the less fortunate. They were willing to give their own toys, shoes, or clothes just to help another child. Could we take on that child-like innocence of helping to be kind and help someone in a loving, innocent way? Children always feel so happy and fulfilled after helping out. Wouldn't it be great for us to experience that fulfillment as well?

~~Anonymous

Give what you have. To someone else
it may be better than you dare to think.
~~Henry Wadsworth Longfellow

More Than A Bystander
A Pass-along Thank You

About three years ago while watching news coverage of the various local and national Veteran's Day celebrations, it suddenly dawned on me that I had never personally thanked any veterans for their sacrifices and contributions to keeping not only our nation but also our world safe.

Sadly, this included my own father, who had served in the U.S. Navy during World War II and later in the Korean War. These generations of soldiers, and the loved ones they left behind on the home front, are rare individuals. They did what their country expected of them, and then returned home, rarely speaking of the horrors they endured and the atrocities they witnessed. I guess I assumed that because I had merely attended veteran celebrations over the years—including Memorial Day flag-raisings and wreath-layings and Veteran's Day parades—that my attendance alone showed my appreciation for their many sacrifices. I decided to be more than just a bystander.

It began with a phone call to my daddy. I thanked him for his service to this country so many years before—service that to this day has insured my freedom and that of my children and grandchildren. Although he was very touched, he was equally stunned. He stated that in "all of his years, no one had ever thanked him before." How sad, but how proud I was that I was the first to do so!

During this year of heightened awareness regarding the lack of recognition toward the soldiers of World War II, and the civilians who served on the home front, I invite everyone to follow my footsteps and thank our veterans.

Senator Bob Dole and Tom Hanks, the actor, have made it painfully aware that this generation of soldiers and civilians have never been honored with the typical memorial. They will finally be recognized when groundbreaking takes place on Veteran's Day this year for the National World War II Memorial in Washington, D.C. Somehow I feel that even though our veterans are thankful for the belated recognition, they would feel equally validated with a heartfelt handshake or a personal "Thank You" just as my father was.

We are presently losing about 1,000 of these veterans each week. Thank God they have been able to live long lives, but it would be an enormous offense if they all left this world without ever receiving personal recognition for their efforts. So, don't just sit back and watch as I did for so many years—thank a veteran today!

Gail Istre

What A Blind Man Hears
The Language of Kindness

I wasn't always blind, so I do know what it's like to see. I'm just not able to see anymore. So you might see me walking with a guide and/or a white walking stick. I feel it is important to mention a few kind things that would help me with my getting around, and help you feel more comfortable with my attempt at getting around, especially if I'm alone.

One of the first things you could do to help me is to remember that my hearing isn't impaired, only my vision, and I really rely on my hearing to make me more aware of my surroundings. If I am walking towards you and you are talking with a friend, don't stop talking just to watch me walk past because I am relying on your voice to judge your distance from me.

When you stop talking, I'm not sure of your location. You may have stopped or stepped aside to let me pass, but I certainly won't notice unless I hear you. If you are walking past me, it's nice if you say "hello" to me because I can hear a smile in your voice.

It isn't necessary to yell loudly at me, as some have the tendency to do, unless of course I am headed towards a ravine or down a flight of stairs. I like to change my course of action if at all possible in a situation like that. The stairs are rarely a problem for me, but as with anyone, they are bet-ter suited for me to walk up or down. I haven't perfected my tumbling skills as of yet! If you are guiding me, as we reach the stairs be sure to tell me if we are going up or down them. This is one time I don't appreciate surprises.

I usually try to walk in places I'm familiar with and often I have someone to guide me, but on occa-sion I must walk alone. I will say some of my guides are better than others (but I won't mention any of the not-so-qualified guides by name). It's funny, though, how many things I can run into when some-one who can see is guiding me, or how many things my guide seems to run into with me by her side. I think that sometimes I would be safer without a guide. (Wouldn't you agree, Kimberly?)

When someone is walking up behind me, I can hear the footsteps, and I know exactly when that person notices me because the quick-paced "step-step" turns into a very slow "steeeeppp-steeeeppp." If you would like to go around me, at this point it would be nice to use the biker's way of communi-cating. Say, "Passing on the left" or something of that nature.

While on vacation in Laughlin, Nevada, the server at a restaurant we visited asked my wife what I would like to eat. I guess she thought it would be difficult for me to make the decision myself. After I order, eating my meal can be very humorous to the aver-age onlooker. I can't be offended if I don't know you're watching, but my protective guides or wife may be offended for me. The only time I notice is when I hear complete silence as people watch me.

Joan Brock, a good friend of mine who suddenly lost her sight a few years ago, had quite an interesting experience herself. Here is her story. After shopping, Joan tried to hand the cashier her credit card and in the attempt to get it to the cashier's hand they kept missing each other. After several attempts Joan finally said, "Since I am blind and can't see your hand, why don't you just take the credit card from me. I will hold my hand still for you." The young cashier said to her, "Oh, then you must know sign language!"

Of course, Joan had to laugh at this statement. She thought to herself that it would be nice to know sign language, but it wouldn't do me much good since I can't see the hands of the person who would be using it to communicate with me because I said "BLIND, not DEAF."

I just thought I would take a brief moment to say being blind makes me do things a little differently and it can be a nuisance, but I try to do all the normal things others do. I even build birdhouses and bird feeders in my garage. I handle the entire project by myself from beginning to end. I use a table saw to cut the wood into the right-sized pieces and assemble them into the final product. Now that's a funny story all on its own—a table saw running in a pitch-dark garage at all hours of the day and night and a blind man running it! What will I think of next?

~~*Chuck Wall, Ph.D.*

I Thought She Didn't Love Me

The kindest thing anyone ever did for me was when my mom gave me up when she was on drugs. When I was about 2 years old, my mom started using crack cocaine. When she saw things getting out of control, she called my grandma and asked her if she could keep me until she got her life together. I was mad at her because I thought she didn't love me. When I got older, I asked my mom why she gave me away, and she said it was because she saw a girl take her baby with her to buy drugs and she did not want to end up doing that same thing with me. She said if she had not given me to grandma that anything could have happened to me. My grandma took good care of me and I still got to stay close with my mom. I live with my mom now and I talk to my grandma every day. I'm glad my mom did that for me because I know she would not have done it if she did not love me. That is the kindest thing anyone ever did for me.

~~Candace Jones, age 11

Receiving A Compliment

A compliment is something that is absolutely free and easy to hand out. It is something that someone can remember, even for a whole lifetime. People love to hear something nice about themselves, their children, or even their belongings. How about handing a few of them out today?

Don't forget that if someone gives you a compliment, don't try to give it back or dispute it. Tell that person "Thank you," because it makes him feel good to hear you respond.

Helping Hand

My sixteen-year-old friend and I were spending the day together one Friday. After renting a couple of videos, we walked outside and I saw a woman screaming on the sidewalk next to the street. Oh God, I thought, what has happened? My friend and I ran over to the woman and we found her little boy on the grass.

There were a few people there and "911" had already been called. One of the bystanders said the boy was having a seizure and was unconscious. Luckily there was a nurse there to help out the child. But the woman, on the other hand, was very upset and on her knees crying. Who could blame her? Her son was lying on the ground motionless with no one to assist or communicate with her. Even though I am too shy to approach people I don't know, I felt I needed to do something. So I got down on my knees, took hold of her hand, and told her that everything was going to be okay. She didn't say anything, but I could feel that she was comforted by my attempt to calm her. It was amazing that I could generate so much positive energy! The boy became conscious and was taken away by ambulance. It felt good to try to attend to the mother's needs since the boy was being taken care of.

If I had one wish, it would be for everyone to have a pause button, enabling him or her to stop, put down the coffee, and smell the roses. I know it was a small thing to do and I can't change the world, but I can and I did offer comfort to someone when she needed it the most.

~~Erica Pape, age 16

Wherever there is a human being,
there is an opportunity for a kindness.
~~Marcus Annaeus Seneca

What Constitutes News: Violence Or Goodness?

O bviously we would have to agree that violence dominates all the local newspaper, television and radio station reports. Doesn't that tell us that something is wrong with this society? That is why it is so important to try even harder to pursue and commit acts of kindness.

Pass It On
A Pass-along Thank You

It was February or March of 1990 and I was eighteen years old, pregnant and unmarried. My baby's father moved into my apartment to help me out when we found out that I was pregnant.

I wasn't working because my boss had asked me to quit my secretarial job because it was in an industrial building and supposedly the fumes would make the baby and me sick. I found a waitress job but that only lasted about three weeks when I passed out and they asked me to leave. I went to work at a 7 Eleven, but in my fifth month of pregnancy I started having contractions and couldn't work any more. I went on disability, but that doesn't provide enough to pay for all of the bills. On top of that the baby's father had also lost his job and had been out of work for about 6 to 8 weeks. We were living off a $300 credit card that was almost maxed out.

Rent was due and we had no food in the house. I didn't know what I was going to do or what was going to become of the baby or me. I was clean and sober at the time, and I went to a meeting at the Alano Club in town. I was telling my friends what was going on in my life and I was so upset.

I knew just about everyone in the program in that county because it was a small town, and anyone I didn't know, my friends knew.

However, a woman with short, dark hair, beautiful blue eyes, about 35 years old whom none of us had ever met before walked up to me after the meeting and asked if she could talk to me for a few minutes. I said, "Sure, what can I do for you?" and we sat down at a table to talk. She said that she listened to me tell my story during the meeting and that she was once in a similar position to the one that I was in and handed me a check for $450. I couldn't believe it! I asked her why she would give me so much money. She said, "Because you need it more than I do. I have also been helped in a time of need. All I want to ask of you is that some day you pass on a kindness to someone who could use your help."

The woman walked in and out of my life so quickly I don't even remember her name. Yet she came to me in time for me to start the ball rolling in a positive direction. I know that she was a true angel. She committed a random act of kindness that I have not forgotten and will not ever forget.

I try to pass on kindness to others whenever I see someone in need. Wherever that nice woman is today, I hope she is happy. I know she is truly blessed because she passed her blessings on to me, and I thank her very much.

Andrea Espinoza

*Be kind for everyone you meet
is fighting a hard battle.*
~~Philo

Here Comes Santa Claus

Traveling during a holiday season can be terrible. I think most would agree with that. Think about it. Long lines, delays, crowds; anxious and impatient adults and children. I try most often to avoid the torture of it all. However, one particular year I had to make an exception. It was Christmas Eve, and my wife and I were on our way to Paducah, Kentucky, to visit our daughter. She had recently moved there from Sacramento, California. The anxiety of preparing for the trip was grueling enough. We packed gifts and prepared the house for our absence, and it was already a hectic period of the year. To make the entire ordeal more fun than torture, I focused on doing something special for my daughter when we arrived in St. Louis, which is the closest major airport to Paducah. It occurred to me that she too would have fought crowds both at the airport and on the road, not to mention that·preparing for company made it a stressful time for her as well. I found an antique Santa outfit and decided to take it with me to make the meeting a fun and special one.

So my wife Gwen and I boarded a Delta flight to St. Louis with Santa suit in tow. Our daughter was going to meet us at the airport. I usually plan some kind of surprise when meeting relatives and friends, and it was particularly fun to plan something when meeting her. On most of our trips I generally enjoy observing other people. During the flight on this busy day, I observed what appeared to be lots of people who were either leaving one family or trying to get to another. It was obviously a sad time for many of them. No one looked terribly happy to be flying that night. Kids were restless and parents were angry. That is when I came up with an idea! I asked the flight attendant if it was okay to do something fun to relieve the tension of many of the passengers. I told her about the Santa suit and that I wanted to start my surprise for my daughter a bit early. The flight attendant checked with the pilot to see if it was okay. Not only did he agree, but he also embellished the idea into an event. I changed into the Santa outfit in that little tiny confined bathroom, which was a feat in itself, and I had with me a small bag of candy canes.

As I was about to exit the bathroom, the pilot announced to the passengers that the plane had just had an encounter causing the airplane to dip a wing...and he actually did dip it. Then he announced that Santa's sleigh had landed on the top of the plane and that Santa had asked permission to board. He prepared the passengers for jolly Old St. Nicholas' arrival. That's when I came out of the bathroom and started going down the aisle greeting all the kids. Oddly enough, adults also said they had been good and mentioned what they wanted for Christmas. I gave everyone candy canes. The child sitting in the seat next to mine was extremely afraid of the jolly old man with a beard. So rather than traumatize him, I/Santa sat in the back of the plane and had a good time talking to the passengers and flight attendants for the rest of the flight. While I was sitting there, a gentleman next to me said he thought it was a really neat idea and asked how many flights I had that day. He thought I was working for the airlines. I said, "I'm not! I just dressed up early because I intended on surprising my daughter in St. Louis." He asked me how old my daughter was and was shocked when I told him she was 23.

When we landed in St. Louis, the flight attendants would not let me deplane until they and the pilots had an opportunity to have a photo with "Santa." I realized then that the employees working on that special day were enjoying my small gift. It felt good to know I had helped make this day more special for them as well. The flight attendants replenished my candy bag with peanuts and Junior Pilot wing pins. They knew I would need something for the trek through the airport and they were right!

Walking down the concourse to the baggage claim area was difficult because I had a terrible case of gout, which affected my ankle. As I limped, several kids asked, "What happened, Santa?" I told them I had fallen out of the sleigh because I wasn't wearing my seatbelt, and I was looking for another flight back to the North Pole to get their gifts and return to pass them out. As I waited for our bags to come out of the turnstiles, I sat on one of the luggage carts. Quite a few kids lined up to sit on my lap, excited to tell me what they wanted for Christmas. I gave them wings and a packet of peanuts and told them I'd see what I could do. About that time my daughter walked by and I yelled out, "HO HO HO, Little Girl." I totally surprised her!

The events of that evening and that trip are remembered fondly. It was fun to try and make others feel happy on a day that many of them didn't want to be traveling. But something else happened that night. How rewarding it was and how wonderful it felt, with so little effort, to put smiles on so many other people's faces. As a personal reflection, I wonder who got the most joy—those receiving the benefit of this distraction, or me seeing the joy of smiling faces? This was, I believe, an example of the benefit of a simple "random act of kindness."

~~Ronald D. Duncan

You cannot do a kindness too soon,
for you never know
how soon it will be too late.

~~Ralph Waldo Emerson

Poetic Kindness

Kindness is a word we toss around,
We give a beggar fifty cents
and think we're heaven bound.

It cannot be measured
in dollars and cents,
It's about what you do...
how your time is spent!

With acts of kindness,
You plant a seed
one that generously spreads
to others in need.

No "Thank you" is needed,
No "Pat on the back,"
Just know that they'll
pass on another kind act.

If you ask what kindness
means to me...
It's like selling lemonade for free!

~~Corris Macon

Save A Seat For Me

I work in the radiology department at a large
hospital where one woman was having x-rays
taken on a daily basis because she was dying from
lung cancer. Each day as I passed her in the hall at
work, I would stop to say "hello" and visit with Mrs.
Lee for just a minute. She always appreciated my
cheery hello, as I appreciated hers. One day I noticed she didn't look like her usual self. Her skin had
started that discoloring process that occurs when
someone is very close to death. I knew in my heart
she wouldn't make it through the week. I mustered
up enough strength to say, "Hello, Mrs. Lee. How are
you feeling today?" I needed to take the opportunity
to try to say something that could comfort her at
such a bad time. Looking at me quite sternly, she
said, "Now I think you can see I'm not doing too well.
So why would you even ask me a question like that?"

"Because you are a very lucky lady, Mrs. Lee!"
I said.

Mrs. Lee replied, "How can a dying old woman
be so lucky?"

As I knelt down beside her, I carefully took her
hand and said, "Well, Mrs. Lee, you are a lucky lady
because you will be in Heaven before I will, and I
have a favor to ask of you when you get there. Do
you think you could you do one favor for me?" Mrs.
Lee looked at me with a sweet smile and a twinkle in
her eye—one that she didn't have when we began
talking—and she said, "I guess I could. What is it you
want me to do?"

"I would like for you to save me a seat right next to you at the big banquet table in Heaven because I want to sit next to you when I get there!" I said. With a huge smile on her face Mrs. Lee said, "I will definitely save you a seat right next to me, Mac." And gesturing with her hand, she patted the seat to the left of her. She had her mind on something positive and I knew she was seeing things a little differently now. We both said our traditional "goodbye" and "see you later" as I went off to finish my work.

A code blue was called not too long after that, and it was called for Mrs. Lee. She died that afternoon, but I know she died with a smile on her face because I took advantage of an opportunity to say hello, and give her some comfort at a difficult time. I lost my own son many years ago and I never want to pass up an opportunity to talk to someone, even under difficult circumstances. I consider it a blessing to have the opportunity to say something kind. I know when I lay down to sleep at night that I have not missed an opportunity to try to make someone feel better if I can help it. I have no regrets in life about what I could have said because I know I have already said it.

~~*Mac*

*The best way to cheer yourself is
to try to cheer somebody else up.*

Mark Twain

The Rally

In the small town of Chemainus, British Columbia, Canada, in September 1999, Donna, one of the town's residents, found herself fighting for her life. She was diagnosed with a rare bone marrow disease called Primary Amyloidosis Al. Her only hope for survival was to undergo a Stem Cell Rescue treatment at The Boston University Medical Center. The estimated cost of the procedure was $61,500.00 U.S. Donna didn't have that kind of money, so the community went to work for her.

They rallied and fought along side her as best they could. They organized the "View Street Garage Sale." The residents dug out furniture, appliances and numerous items they had tucked away, dusted them off and put them up for sale. There was food and games for the kids. People came in droves not only from this small town but from nearby towns and the surrounding valley as well. Cars and trucks lined the street. It was a huge success, and on this beautiful day kissed by sunshine and blue skies these caring people raised $12,300.00. It was the first of many fundraisers for Donna.

Unfortunately, Donna lost her battle, but she will long be remembered for bringing a community together to help one of its own.

~~Anonymous

Unsolicited Kindness
A Pass-along Thank You

While visiting in England with my husband and daughter, we decided to go and see *The Lady Is Not for Burning* in Coventry. It starred Richard Chamberlain, who had been a former acting school student and friend of mine, and he was expecting us.

We had a rental car and left from Kent one early Saturday morning. We had traveled about half way when the car decided to be naughty and stopped. We did not know what to do since we were on a long, typically narrow English road with high shrubs on either side. There was no traffic to speak of, and cell phones were not the thing at the time.

While we sat and agonized about the time and about how we were going to get out of this mess, a truck with three men stopped, and they inquired if they could do anything to help us. This act was completely unsolicited and we were grateful that they were able to discover the gas pedal line had snapped. While they didn't have a part to fix it, they pieced together some things from their truck and soon had the ailing car on its way. They knew the remedy was only temporary, so they insisted on accompanying us to the closest town, which had a gas station. Upon our arrival, my husband and I asked if we could pay them for their assistance or buy them something to eat or anything that might show our gratitude. Oddly, they seemed uncomfortable with the offer and they left hurriedly.

We called Richard at the theater and he made reservations for us for the following evening. Such hospitality is memorable, and I have since realized that many people commit a kindness for the sake of the deed and not for an expected reward, and that is the way it should be.

We will always have warm thoughts for these gentlemen who truly understood the meaning of kindness.

Robie Lester Eccleston

No Words

After having an extremely difficult day because of family problems I was dealing with, I had to take a break from my job because I could not stop crying. I was sitting on a bench outside, trying to think things through, not realizing how obviously upset I appeared to passers-by. One woman looked directly at me as she walked past, and then turned around and started walking towards me. Without saying a word she reached out and gave me a loving, consoling hug. Even though no words passed between us, the warmth of her kindness did, and it was exactly what I needed. This caring gesture sent me into a tailspin of a whole different kind of tears, and put a smile in my heart.

~~Laura Besst

Twenty-Dollar Return

I t was a cold Christmas day; the air was filled with moisture. My wife and I were getting ready to have a barbecue. As I went to take out the garbage, I noticed there were two men who looked homeless out by the trash bin. I could see that they were eating something they had no doubt found in the bin. I didn't have the heart to say anything to disturb them or maybe embarrass them. It gave me a lonely, sick feeling inside. Did they even know it was Christmas Day? Don't they have a family somewhere?

They spotted me but they didn't hide. As a matter of fact, it looked as if they were going to guard that bin. I went inside and told my wife about them, then returned back outside and asked if they wanted to join us for dinner. They didn't answer while they cleaned what looked like chicken bones from the garbage. I asked them not to leave, and I went back inside to get my wife. We went to the store and purchased two of the biggest New York steaks that we could find and hurried home.

I started the fire and went out to look for the men. I found them not too far down the alley at another can. I asked them to come with me and we would cook dinner for them, but there was no response. I went home and left the gate open while I cooked the steaks. They finally did show up, but they were reluctant to come in the gate and looked more scared than we were. They sat in a corner of the yard. We made them a plate, and as they ate, they said nothing. They looked as if they were guarding it with their lives, never taking their eyes off me.

My wife was scared when I asked if they wanted to clean themselves up and try some of my clothes on. One of the men got up and left; the other just stood there saying nothing. I coaxed him into the house, gave him some clothes and a couple of razors and a towel. The smell was not pleasant, but nothing could surpass the feeling of happiness when he finally cracked what looked like a smile. It was amazing! He emerged from that bathroom as a different man! He looked as if he were forty years younger and a completely different person. He started to talk but not too much. He said his name was John, and that he had family in Michigan but he hadn't seen them in twenty years. We gave him some more food and he said that he could make it on his own and didn't need help from anyone. I gave him a jacket with a twenty-dollar bill tucked in the pocket and watched him as he walked away. I thought how good my clothes looked on him—such a perfect fit! Although I never saw him come back, later in the day I found that twenty-dollar bill under an empty can on my front porch.

Merry Christmas, John, and good luck!

~~Kevin Handy

Furry Friend

There is a truly special lady who lives in my neighborhood. Her name is Patsy and she spends a great deal of her time volunteering at the local elementary schools, the Chamber of Commerce, the humane society, and numerous other organizations.

Late one Sunday afternoon while my in-laws were visiting from out of state, a stray cat appeared at my door in the obvious stages of late labor. We were on our way out and had an appointment that we had to keep. So I knew just where to take her—to Patsy's house! With a quick explanation of the situation, I handed the cat over. Patsy immediately made her a bed in a carrier, and went straight to work on the phone to find her a "foster" home. Within minutes our furry friend was bedded down in a cozy bed, delivered four beautiful and healthy kittens and was placed in a temporary home. Patsy named her "Olivia," and already had several leads for homes for the kittens.

When the time comes, Patsy will take her to the veterinarian and pay for her to be spayed, tested for viruses and vaccinated. She has done this for many, many cats in our neighborhood and pays the expenses out of her own pocket. When we returned home, I went to Patsy's home to thank her for her kindness. It was a nice surprise when she thanked me for bringing the "mom-to-be" to her home. As I walked away, I thought who else but Patsy would thank someone for showing up at her door unannounced with a pregnant cat in mid-labor. She is a selfless person, and I truly believe that to see the kindness in someone's heart, you only need to look at the way they treat animals!

~~*Sara Woodall*

Make Contact

A chiropractor I once worked for said, "I realize that sometimes I am the only person who makes physical contact with an elderly person in a month's time. Physical contact is very important to all of us. So I try to make some form of contact with my elderly patients especially even if it's only to place my hand on their shoulder while we talk." Do you have a lonely loved one in need of attention?

It's not just the elderly who are lonely; young people can be lonely, too. Some teenagers would love their parents to just grab them and hug them for no reason. Can you do that today? If it feels awkward to do, then do it awkwardly, but just do it. It is better to have an awkward hug than no hug at all. Never miss an opportunity you may not get again. Life is unpredictable and short.

~~*Anonymous*

The Salute

Having served in World War II as a tail gunner on a B-17 Flying Fortress attached to the 8th Air Force, 34th Bombardment Group stationed in Mendlesham, England, I have a special license plate that was made for the front of my automobiles. The plates read "8th Air Force 34th Bomb Group" and display replicated pictures of the B-17 Flying Fortress and the B-24 Liberator Bomber. One day after shopping at a local establishment, I encountered a young man standing in front of my car looking at my license plate. As I approached and started to enter my automobile, he said, "Sir, I just want to thank you for serving our country and I salute you."

At that he promptly gave me a snappy salute, which I returned to him, bringing tears to the eyes of this old soldier.

~~Herman Fieber,
Former Sergeant, U.S. Army-Air Force

The story you just read is a notably memorable incident experienced by my husband. After church one Sunday afternoon as I was entering my automobile with a matching license plate, I found a note on the windshield saying, "We want to thank you for all the things you have done for this great country of ours!" My husband has carried wounds for fifty years as a result of his plane crashing. Sentiments such as this note are a constant reminder of his sacrifice and bring tears to my eyes each time.

~~Nancy Fieber

A Biblical Perspective On Kindness

K indness is a word that is found many times in the Bible. There are nearly twice as many references in the Old Testament as in the New Testament, and I discovered in doing a word study that "kindness" has a much deeper meaning to us today than in the New Testament.

The Old Testament use of kindness often describes an attribute of God. Some examples are loving kindness, merciful kindness, everlasting kindness, abundant kindness, etc.

It is also a word that can be substituted for loyalty, as in II Samuel 10. Kindness was returned for kindness (or loyalty for loyalty) between King David and Hanun. Most of the Old Testament scriptures about kindness refer to a kindness being returned. Joseph requested a kindness from the cupbearer for whom he interpreted a dream. This eventually resulted in his release from prison and his rise to second most powerful ruler in Egypt. Rahab showed kindness to the Israelite spies and it resulted in her and her entire family being spared the destruction of Jericho. In the book of Ruth, Boaz showed kindness to Ruth and Naomi, which resulted in him becoming Naomi's kinsman redeemer. This kindness was a return to Ruth for her amazing loyalty and kindness to her mother-in-law. Ruth's position in history became quite significant as a result of her kindness. She was the great-grandmother of King David into whose lineage Jesus was born many generations later.

There are also examples of entire peoples who

had kindness returned to them because of good things they had done. The people of Jabesh-Gilead who rescued the body of King Saul and gave it a proper burial (in II Samuel) which resulted in King David praying to the God of Israel to show them kindness and truth for their actions. The story of Esther gives us another slant on kindness. She was extended kindness (also translated favor) by the king. This kindness extended to Esther resulted in her being given the opportunity to save her people from destruction and the king gaining God's favor for his own people. Many people would have died or suffered terribly had that initial act of kindness not been offered.

Proverbs is God's book of wisdom. Proverbs 19:22 describes what is desired in man: loyalty and kindness. These are great attributes. In Proverbs 31:26 a virtuous woman is described as one who "opens her mouth with wisdom and on her tongue is the law of kindness."

Finally, there are three scriptures that describe the attributes of God the same. They are Exodus 34:6, Joel 2:13, and Jonah 4:2. These say that God is gracious, merciful, slow to anger and of great kindness.

The New Testament differs from the Old Testament in that kindness is a fruit of the spirit. It describes love as being kind, or said another way, one of love's expressions is kindness. Those individuals who have cast off their old sinful nature and taken on the nature of Christ are told that with this comes kindness for one another, tender-heartedness, compassion, understanding, and readiness to forgive. In Luke 6 Jesus is teaching a large group of followers. He begins to teach them some very revolutionary lessons for that day and time. These lessons included how to treat their neighbors and their enemies, in particular. I say they were revolutionary because they went beyond the Law of Moses and required a change of "heart." His instructions included loving their enemies, doing good to those who hate you, blessing those who curse you, and praying for those who despitefully use you. This is how God operates and how He wants us to operate. Verse 35 says, *"But love your enemies, do good and lend, hoping for nothing in return, and your reward will be great and you will be sons of the Most High. For He is kind to the unthankful and evil."*

Colossians 3:12 lists Christ-like attributes given to the elect of God: *"Put on tender mercies, kindness, humility, meekness, longsuffering (patience), a forgiving spirit, above all, put on love, which is a bond of perfection, let peace rule your heart, be thankful, let the words of Christ dwell in you in wisdom, teach and admonish one another in worship, and do all you do in the name of the Lord."*

The Bible has a lot to say about kindness. It is a very important attribute of God and can result in the most amazing things when one who has received it from you gives a return of kindness. It is also a fruit of the spirit, which includes love, joy, peace, patience, kindness, goodness, faithfulness, gentleness, and self-control.

Be kind one to another for the Lord God has been kind to you. It could result in a benefit when you least expect it. God bless you.

~~Mary Poehner

Compassion • Patience • Humility • Respect • Consideration •

The Kindness Recipe

2 heaping hands full of **Patience**

1 large heart full of **Humility**

1 palm full of **Dignity**

1 part **Respect** from giver;
1 part from receiver

Heaping amounts of **Consideration**

Compassion - melted down and mixed carefully

Appreciation - massive amounts

Tolerance - an infinite amount

Mix patience, humility, dignity and respect with love and tenderness.

Add compassion, consideration, appreciation, and tolerance.

Gently fold with pride and conviction.

Add self-esteem and knead (need) carefully.

Bake at 98.6° for life.

Sprinkle with joy and serve daily with a smile to friends and strangers.

Compassion • Patience • Humility • Respect • Consideration

What Is Kindness To You?

Each and every person on earth has his or her own definition for what kindness is. What is your definition of kindness? Do you ever feel like going out and committing a senseless act of kindness yourself? If so, you are not alone. There are many individuals throughout the world feeling the same as you. Sometimes, though, we have a tendency not to act on that urge. Instead, we experience good things through listening or reading about someone else's experience. But what if we took the time to act upon our own kind thoughts? We just might have too many happy people in this world. We could witness some of these wonderful things first hand.

Premeditate your kind act as soon as possible so we can all share in this wonderful learning experience!

Sacrificial Piano

A few years ago I worked in the office of an oncology medical practice for a physician, Dr. Roberts. He was a renowned and respected member of the medical community, but known for a "poor bedside manner." However, a story that circulated throughout the office grapevine showed he was actually a kind-hearted man. Dr. Roberts had a great number of cancer patients, but he had one patient in particular who was not obtaining the desired results from the chemotherapy treatments she was receiving. He informed his patient, Linda, that there was a new drug available that she might benefit from.

But it was extremely expensive and was not covered by her insurance. Because of the expense of the drug, she came face to face with the only option she had—selling her prized possession, her grand piano. She thought long and hard before deciding what to do, but Linda knew that selling the piano was the only option that could possibly help save her life. She had to take that chance. Maybe someone else would love her piano as much as she did, and maybe they would even benefit from her sacrifice. At least that was the idea she comforted herself with.

Miraculously, Linda recovered from her cancer treatment. Thankful to have survived, and appreciating her life like never before, she opted to move to another town to gain a new perspective on her second chance at life. Dr. Roberts, a music lover himself, received great pleasure from the symphonies that he attended. He could only imagine what a sacrifice it must have been for Linda to sell something she was talented enough to play and to part with something that was so important to her. He was so pleased with her recovery, her positive attitude and her strength to survive that he purchased a grand piano for Linda and gave it to her before she moved away. Now these two music lovers' hearts have been touched by an act of kindness so genuine that any music they hear must have an even sweeter sound than it did before.

~~Di Wall

Four Hands

As a fourteen-year-old teenager, I think kindness is choosing to help my grandmother cook dinner for 260 to 300 elderly people instead of hanging out with my friends. We cook seven to ten turkeys or hams, mashed potatoes, green beans and pretty much anything else you can think of to make a full-course meal. Because my grandma is so stubborn, if she doesn't have anyone to help her with the meal, she will do it all herself. She feels guilty having her holiday dinner knowing others may go without. This is her holiday ritual and when she is finished, she has blisters and cuts all over her hands and is exhausted to death. When I am at her house helping out, it's nice to see my two hands working right beside her two hands. This big job becomes twice as easy for her with four hands to do the work.

~~*Amber Adams*

Analyze Ourselves

Isn't it something how we can always find fault with someone else and not usually with ourselves? Have you ever found yourself looking for a book to buy to give advice to a friend or family member? What about the book that will help you? What about the advice you could give to yourself? We must analyze the things we say and do and our motives behind them before we can try to benefit others in a constructive way. Are we being the best that we can be? And if not, what can we do to change ourselves?

The Bad Year
A Pass-along Thank You

On Feb. 9, 1995, we had a house fire and lost almost everything we owned. To make matters worse, in April of the same year my husband, James, was killed in a car accident on the way home from work. We had three children and not a lot of money, and were still trying to recover from the fire. Our small community got together at our children's school and took up collections that helped with the funeral expenses and all of the bills I was left to pay alone. The teachers and counselors came to our home and to the funeral to support and check on the children. We received a tremendous amount of support from complete strangers. Even the youngest school-aged children were helping out and making cards to encourage us. These grim experiences were made so much better because of the kindness and support of others. It is amazing to think how much someone can make a difference in your life.

Kelly Burke
Olathe, Kansas

Compassion is the basis for all morality.
~~Arthur Schopenhauer

Earthly Angels
A Pass-along Thank You

I had only been on my new job for a month when unexpectedly I found out I was pregnant with twins. I was still in my probationary period at work, and my husband and I didn't know what we were going to do if I lost my job due to the pregnancy. We already had two children, ages two and four years old. We had also just purchased a car so we had extra monthly payments to make and we were already struggling financially. I also worried about how we would pay for the doctor's visits and hospital bills without the insurance from my new job.

I knew I had to inform my boss as soon as possible. Phil, a man from our church, had hired me but he was under no obligation to keep me. Expecting the worst, I broke the news to him. Was I in for a shock! Not only did Phil tell me everything was going to be fine and not to worry about anything, but he also encouraged me in a positive way about all of my numerous other concerns. He provided me with emotional support and encouraging emails and "how-to" advice on dealing with difficult situations.

About two months into my job I became so ill I was unable to work at all. I was put on home rest with intravenous antibiotics and fluid because I couldn't keep any food or liquid down. Even though I was thankful not to be fired, this brought a whole new set of problems. I found out I was not eligible for disability benefits, and once again Phil came to our rescue. He hired someone to work in my place while I was gone, and I received sub-differential pay, which allowed me to keep the insurance benefits. Our church followed Phil's lead and we received many wonderful acts of kindness. Through the kindness and generosity of others, my family and I made it.

Thanks to Phil, I was able to stay on the company's insurance plan because he kept me on at work, and I received some pay from my job so that we could pay our bills. Phil also held my position for me so I could go back to work after I had the twins.

When I had to stop working because of my problem pregnancy, Christine, my neighbor and nurse, helped me at all hours of the day and night to administer the intravenous antibiotics I needed. Regina, my best friend, would come over and wash my hair since I couldn't do it myself.

Church members brought meals to our home for two weeks after I came home with the twins and provided all the utensils, food and drinks. They helped us take care of the twins, our other two children, and performed other needed chores.

I want to thank God and all of his earthly angels who helped us during such a difficult time in our lives.

Kristi Long

Like Father, Like Son

O ne day while I was dining at a local restaurant, a young girl, who was struggling with her walker as she passed my table, surprisingly took the time to flash a sweet smile that brightened my day. The client I was dining with happened to know the family, so I had a beautiful pearl necklace delivered to her home, thanking her for the pleasant smile that warmed my heart. I believe it is important to appreciate all the small things in life such as a smile or a laugh. Many times people take these things for granted. The father of the young girl, in appreciation for my gift, brought the young girl into my store wearing a new dress, her pearl necklace, and most of all her sweet smile.

Needless to say, my wife and I tried to instill good morals and values into our own children by raising them to be aware of other people's needs. So I couldn't have been happier when out of the blue I received a phone call from someone inquiring about my own son, who had committed a random act of kindness. I was pleased to hear my son had actually learned something from "good old dad." I know now that the values I tried to pass on to my children have been passed on as examples to their children and my grandchildren. This shows me that generational acts of kindness can be committed. I am a very proud parent. The following story will tell you about my son, Jon Hall, and what he did for Judge Hoover and a man named Jimmy.

~~*Don Hall*

The Chain Reaction

J udge Hoover is the judge presiding over a drug court program. He works very closely with individuals who have abused drugs and ultimately ended up in the court system. Some of the people in the program do very well and eventually lead a clean and sober life. At least that is what the program is designed to do—help encourage and train its participants about living drug-free. Judge Hoover has committed many acts of kindness in his years of service presiding in this court, but this story happens to be the one that we were told about, and we decided to share it with you. This is a perfect example of how people can be touched with one small beginning, thus causing "a chain reaction."

Judge Hoover dealt with a man, Jimmy S., in the court system off and on for years. Jimmy always wore a thick gold chain, but Judge Hoover noticed he wasn't wearing it the last time he appeared in court. He asked Jimmy where his trademark chain was. He said that he had broken the chain and didn't have enough money to have it fixed yet. Jimmy was working on straightening out his life and had been clean for three years when a slight mishap brought him before Judge Hoover again. Judge Hoover asked Jimmy to bring him the chain and he would check into getting it fixed at a reasonable price for him. Judge Hoover took the chain to his friend, a local jeweler, Jon Hall...

The Chain Reaction Continues

This is the act of kindness that we were told Jon Hall committed. This is Jon's side of the story.
Judge Hoover, a friend of mine, brought me a broken chain that belonged to one of the clients from his drug program. After explaining to me how hard this man had worked on straightening out his life, I decided I wanted to fix the chain for the man free of charge. I was happy to hear what attempts Jimmy had made at keeping his life drug free after so many years of abuse, and I wanted to help him out if I could. Here is the touching letter I received from Jimmy S. It made me happy that he appreciated my efforts.

Mr. Jon Hall,
You don't know me but you have blessed me very much. My name is Jimmy S., and I was a heroin addict for 36 years. I had made a change in my life and became a Christian 3 years ago, but a few months ago I messed up and to make a long story short I ended up in Judge Hoover's court. I have been through the system in and out of jail and prison and I've never met a judge like Hoover!
My wife and I both work but we could not afford to have a gold chain I had broken repaired. Judge Hoover kindly offered to have it fixed for me and with your help it's like new.
I thank you from the bottom of my heart

for your kindness to me. I never knew there were men like you and Judge Hoover who would care about a drug addict like me. Your Kindness makes me even more determined to stay clean. I thank my God for you, Jon Hall. You will never realize how much you have touched my life.

Sincerely, Jimmy S.

~~Jon Hall

Listen Up!

Do you consider yourself to be a good listener? I believe that if you really listen to the person speaking and do not speak for five full seconds after the speaker is finished, we will have better listeners in this world. I call this the five-second-pause technique.

Pay close attention to what the person is saying, not to what you want to say next. We all get in a hurry to say as much as we can as fast as we can in this speedy world we live in.

Let's give it a try and really listen. Then try to recall what the person has just finished saying. Were you listening well enough to remember?

~~ Chuck Wall, Ph.D.

Whisper Voice

This is a story that my friend told me and it has changed my life forever. My friend, Lisa, called an elderly friend of the family. When the woman answered the phone, her voice was as quiet as a whisper. Lisa asked the woman if she was sick because she sounded so quiet when she answered the phone. The elderly woman said she was not sick, but if she hasn't spoken all day, that's what her voice sounds like when she speaks for the first time. Can you imagine being alone and not speaking to anyone on the phone or in person all day long, sometimes for days? This story made me so sad that it changed the way I do things. I schedule my day to include at least one phone call to someone who could really use it. It makes me feel as if I have accomplished something good in my day, and it only takes a few minutes to brighten someone else's day. Sometimes even the people we think are the strongest are the very ones who could use a phone call.

~~*Dana*

*There is no greater loan
than a sympathetic ear.*
~~*Frank Tyger*

I Bought This For You!
A Pass-along Thank You

One day just before Mother's Day, I was with my husband at a garden center shopping for flowers for our front yard. Since I retired some years ago, I enjoy sitting in the front yard looking at them. I carefully selected each one. When I was finished making my choices, I went to the checkout stand to pay for them. I waited patiently as I stood in line next to a woman that had a Red Flyer wagon full of flowers. She was giving the clerk instructions so that her husband could come back later that evening and pick them up for her. As I was paying for my flowers, I saw the woman pick up another pot from outside and bring it to the clerk who had been helping her. I overheard the woman asking the clerk to add this new pot to her bill. As I was leaving the store, the woman, probably about the same age as my own daughter, handed me this beautiful double yellow hibiscus. She said, "I bought this plant for you. I saw you looking at it earlier and I thought you should have it. I hope you don't mind, but you remind me of someone very dear to me who lives in Texas, and I don't get to see her often enough. Please accept it." It was so beautiful! Because it was so close to Mother's Day, maybe I reminded her of her mother and my accepting the plant would make her happy. I know how it feels being far away from loved ones. I took the plant and thanked the woman for her kind gesture. That plant grows in a pot in my front yard and is even more beautiful simply because someone wanted to please me.

Helena Verheaghe

A Childhood Lesson

Overnight the mountains were covered with about ten inches of snow. The pass going to Medford was a nightmare and some folks got caught without snow tires or chains. We had taken a drive that day so our kids could play in the snow when we came across a couple whose car was stuck in a snow bank. Since we had a 4-wheel drive and a winch, we attempted to pull them out. Our boys had to wade in waist-deep snow to hook up the cable from the winch, but after much struggle the couple's car was freed. They tried to pay us for our help but my husband Ron said, "Merry Christmas" and they went on their way. That day we pulled many vehicles out of the snow only to end up later stuck ourselves. Fortunately a good samaritan stopped to help pull us out. Not only did we all feel good about the help we gave and the help we received, but also this childhood lesson helped teach the boys about good deeds and the benefit of hard work. Our kids were about 6, 9 and 10 years old and they had a ball helping people out. To this day they are still very good at offering a helping hand and they have fond memories of that day.

~~Carol and Ron Biles
Klamath Basin

The Offer

It was Thanksgiving Day when my husband had to go to the emergency room. His leg was swollen and he was in extreme pain. Though the nursing staff was very kind to me, I had no family or friends to help me cope with my feelings of fear and helplessness. I stayed with him at the hospital for five days until the blood clots had been dissolved and it seemed that he would survive.

When I returned "home," our neighbors, Carol and Ron Biles, immediately greeted me. I don't know them well, but their motor home is parked in the space next to our 5th wheel. Like all good neighbors, they wondered if we were gone or had suffered some misfortune.

I explained to them what happened, and they showed genuine care and compassion. They offered to do anything they could to help me. Though I had no task that required help, the offer of help and their friendship was the help I needed.

Their *offer* was the kind deed.

~~Carol Parker

Whose Responsibility Is It?

Whose responsibility is it to help others in need—yours or mine? We have a tendency to look to someone else to do the work of helping others who need it. Yet it is the responsibility of all of us to help others.

What if someone were in need of just a kind word

or action? If we knew in advance that someone needed it, would it be easier to act upon? Do we need someone to hold up a sign that says, "I need attention?" What if we knew an act of kindness could save a life? In this difficult world we live in people look forward to coming in contact with smiling, loving faces. What is it that goes through someone's head just before he commits suicide? We don't know. But what if we had said "hello" or smiled at that person, and it was just the positive experience he needed to help him make a better decision? I know of several instances where an individual was going to commit suicide and just because someone knocked on the door or called him on the phone it stopped him from doing so. We should assume all people are carrying a sign asking for kindness and give away our kindness to them as freely as we can.

The smartest thing I ever said was, "Help Me!"
                                    ~~Anonymous

How To Communicate With The Deaf
The Language of Kindness

*"Blindness cuts us off from things.
Deafness cuts us off from people."*
            ~~Helen Keller

As a hearing daughter raised in a deaf family and community, I know how difficult communicating across cultures can be. Through my own experience I understand that it is natural to feel uncomfortable when trying to communicate with someone whose language is different from our own. Many times our biggest worry is that we will feel stupid and in turn make the other person feel uncomfortable because of our awkwardness. Here are six simple tips that I've found to make communicating with someone deaf more effective.

1. Before you speak make sure you have the deaf person's attention. You can do this with a tap on the shoulder or arm, a wave, a smile or another visual cue.

2. Look directly at the deaf person and make eye contact. This allows him to clearly read your face and lips. Additionally, eye contact allows a direct communication connection to be made. Even if an interpreter is present, speak directly to the deaf person. He will turn to the interpreter as needed.

3. Ask the deaf person the best way to communicate. He may prefer to write or to move to a location where he can see you more clearly. Or he may choose to use another person to interpret for him.

4. When speaking, use short sentences and talk slowly and clearly. Please don't yell, exaggerate or over pronounce. If you are writing, keep your sentences short and concise. Don't be afraid to use pantomime, body language, gestures and facial expressions to get your point across.

5. If you're not being understood, first repeat, then rephrase your message. Repetition allows the deaf person to catch missed words. However, some combinations of lip movements are difficult to lip read and rephrasing alleviates that.

6. Finally, be patient with yourself as well as the person with whom you're communicating.

Remember, whenever you choose to step out of your comfort zone to make a connection with someone, you are exercising an act of kindness, and that goes a long way in bridging any communication gap.

~~*Dr. A.C. Malinowski*

As a consultant and national motivational speaker, Dr. Malinowski has reached out to over 250,000 people with her work in the area of diversity and communication training. As an actor and writer, she performs with the award-winning, nationally touring, multi-cultural show "A Slice of Rice, Frijoles, Greens" which builds cultural bridges through the arts.

Hey! That's My Wheelchair!

My father-in-law, Bill, was taking me home after helping him repair his wheelchair late one afternoon. He drives a Plymouth Voyager which is equipped with hand controls because he had to have one of his legs amputated some years ago. We put the repaired wheelchair into the back of his Voyager and we were on the way to my house when we stopped at a red light. As Bill started driving through the intersection, the hatchback on the Voyager opened up and the wheelchair fell out of the back of it and landed in the intersection. He pulled over so I could pick up the chair from the road. While I waited for an opportunity to step into the intersection to get the wheelchair, a man in a white pick-up truck traveling through the intersection opened the door of his truck, scooped up the chair, and set it beside him in his truck. I was shocked and could not believe my eyes! It was obvious that I was waiting for a clear moment to pick up the wheelchair from the intersection. A young man in a blue car driving in the opposite direction of the truck happened to witness the incident. Realizing the man had just stolen the wheelchair, he yelled out his window to me, "Is that your wheelchair that man just took?"

I yelled back, "Yes, it is."

The young man shouted back me, "Stay right there and I'll be righ back with your wheelchair!" He made a U-turn and followed the man in the white truck. After a few minutes, the man in the blue car came back to where we were parked, waving his arms and yelling to us, "I got it! I got your wheelchair!"

I don't know how he got it back and I didn't ask, but we all shook hands and we thanked him. He said that he had friends who were in the wheelchair business and he knew how expensive they were, so he just wanted to help us if he could. He was a clean-cut man in his early 20's, and we certainly appreciated his help. He truly restored my faith in young people in this day and time. I was proud to see the younger generation help out the older generation.

~~Patrick Nolan

Slipping In Some Kindness

You know how it feels to slip your chilly feet into a cozy pair of warm fuzzy slippers? That is what it's like slipping a little kindness into your heart or letting a little kindness slip out of your heart each and every day. Not only will you feel good about the cozy feeling you carry within you, but also others will feel it coming from you.

There is no greater joy than to know the feeling of doing something good for others. It can be the smallest or largest act of kindness committed that could make a difference in someone else's life. This book will show you that kindness comes in all shapes and sizes, just like our hearts. Some are very large and some are very small, but all work together to accomplish one goal. If we could set one goal for our hearts, then let's make that one goal kindness.

Secret Agent

I t was mid-December and one of our company's managers was interviewing people to fill several positions in our manufacturing plant. He interviewed an applicant whose situation touched his heart. Her name was Sara and she was a young, single mom with two small children. Her work history was poor and indicated that she had not worked at any job for more than a couple of months at a time. At the end of the interview she asked when she would receive her first paycheck if she were to get hired. She wanted to provide a Christmas celebration for her children and was hoping that she could get paid prior to Christmas. He explained to her that even if she were to start work the next day, she would not receive any pay until after Christmas. Sara was clearly disappointed, and because of her poor work history she did not get the job.

After Sara left his office, the manager couldn't get her or her predicament out of his mind. Imagine not being able to provide for your children—particularly at Christmas! He wrote down her name and phone number because he knew that if he put his mind to it, he could somehow help with her Christmas dilemma. There were two things to consider--it was important to keep any connection with his company separate from his personal desire to help her, and he would need someone to help with his project.

He shared Sara's story with his wife Betty, and she couldn't wait to be his "accomplice." They worked out all the details of their soon-to-be kindness mission and everything went like clockwork.

Here's what they did.

His wife contacted Sara and identified herself only as Betty. She explained to Sara that she had been told of her situation and had a solution to her Christmas dilemma. Betty told her she would be willing to assist her in a shopping spree for the children if she would meet her at KMart at a designated time. Sara enthusiastically agreed.

When Sara arrived, she had both children "in tow." She and Betty visited briefly, and then Betty took the children to the snack bar so their mother could shop for gifts. Sara was given instructions to fill up a shopping cart full of whatever she thought would make her children's Christmas a special one. When she was finished, Sara was to discreetly flash Betty a specific signal so Betty could assume the payment position. After the merchandise was paid for, Sara took the merchandise to the trunk of her car, placing it carefully out of the prying eyes of her children, thus preserving their upcoming surprise.

When Sara came back in for her children, she asked what organization Betty was with and where she could send a thank-you card. Betty replied that this was a top-secret Christmas mission and under no circumstances could she divulge that information, but that the message would be passed on to her superiors. Knowing Sara and her children would have a Christmas was the only thanks necessary.

These two "secret agents" had an extra special Christmas that year knowing that they were able to pull off a secret mission of helping someone in need.

~~*Charlette Sears*
Temple, Texas

Choices
The Language of Kindness

I spent twenty-two years in the military, a good portion of which was as a medical evacuation helicopter pilot. During my military career, I witnessed numerous traumatic results that war can have on the human body. Even though I am now retired from the military, I have found that life sometimes forces you to make some serious choices about the circumstances you are faced with each day.

About a year ago I went into the hospital for a knee replacement, but complications set in and my right leg had to be amputated. When this happened, there were some serious choices that I had to make. I could choose to be depressed by feeling sorry for myself, or I could choose to get back to living a normal life again. Fortunately, I've been blessed with a strong constitution, a positive attitude, and a supportive family. All of these factors helped me to overcome my ordeal. Three months after the surgery I was fitted for a prosthetic leg, and with the help of family and friends I've been able to resume my normal life style.

As I reflect on this experience, the hardest thing to understand was how other people dealt with my problem. Recently my own brother confided that when I lost my leg he didn't know what to say or how to talk to me, and just the other day a close friend reiterated that he felt the same way. In retrospect, I can understand people being sensitive to my feelings because they were not sure how I was dealing with my new problem. However, I would have thought all of these people knew me well enough to understand that losing my leg wouldn't change me as a person. I'm still the same person I have always been. I'm just thirty-five pounds lighter and I wear a prosthetic leg!

Some people have a tendency to back away from me when we're talking as if I have a contagious disease. I even had one individual yelling in my ear. He seemed quite embarrassed when I told him that I'd only lost my leg, not my hearing. The most difficult thing to deal with is when people you associated with prior to the incident now deliberately avoid you. Then you really find out who your friends are.

If there is one thing that should be stressed about people with a physical limitation, it is that everyone should strive to recognize a physical limitation for exactly what it is—a limitation. As a result of my situation, I now must be a little more aware of how I do things. However, by maintaining a positive attitude I stay focused on the most important issues in my life. Remember—I'm the same person, and hopefully you'll choose to treat me with respect and dignity. If you do, then we will get along just fine.

~~Chuck Broughton

Kristin's Journey

Fifteen years ago I was teaching 8th grade. One of my students was a bright and beautiful girl named Kristin. She was a typical young teenager—very talkative, full of life, humor, and independence. She exhibited all of the emotions of a growing teenage girl—boyfriend joys and woes, behaving very adult-like one day and wanting to be comforted like a small child the next.

Not only was Kristin in my social studies class, she was also in my homeroom. Several times a week she wrote in a private journal that only she and I shared. She would write and I would respond. She shared her thoughts, joys, and frustrations, yet she seldom acknowledged my responses. After all it wasn't "cool" to really like teachers.

One morning Kristin's friends arrived at school crying and inconsolable. They informed me that she had been struck by a car the night before and was in the hospital. I immediately called the hospital to check on her and was connected to her room. Her mother answered the telephone. When I told her my name, I was completely surprised at her response. She burst into tears and told me how glad she was I called because I was Kristin's favorite teacher! She told me that Kristin was on life support and the prognosis was not a good one. I kept in touch with her several times during that day, and when I called the next morning, she shared with me that she had to make the unbearable decision to take her daughter off life support. She went on to say that she wanted Kristin's life to continue on in others, so she decided to donate her organs. This was an extraordinary gesture since it was not a customary practice fifteen years ago!

I visited Kristin's mother during those terrible days and after the funeral I met with her again. I wanted to give her Kristin's journal. At least when she would read it, she could share what had been important to Kristin at that time in her brief life, and it was a part of Kristin that she could cherish through the years. She gratefully clutched the journal to her heart and thanked me after I handed it to her. Both of us were crying. At that moment I told her that her decision to donate Kristin's organs had changed my life—I decided to become an organ donor! I am forever committed to life after life because of one young girl who touched me, and now Kristen's journey of life lives on in others.

~~Nancy Packard

We're On The Right Track

There can be a downside to kindness. After a seemingly simple assignment to my students to "go out, commit a random act of senseless kindness and then write an essay about your good deed," I found it rather disturbing that some of the students were having a difficult time trying to commit their act of kindness. When people were approached, they were fearful of the students' initial intentions. Some of them were rejected completely and some were allowed to commit their kind act, but only under caution and scrutiny.

Because we are not a society of people viewing kindness as a necessity, people become suspicious of others who want to go out of their way to do something kind. The kind act someone wants to commit can lose some of its enjoyment because of that suspicion.

It proves to me that we are on the right track! We need more kindness in the world today. Of course, you don't need me to tell you that. But be warned that you may run across this strange phenomenon yourself. Do not let it discourage you! Let it make you stronger and more zealous about committing your acts of kindness.

~~Chuck Wall, Ph.D.

The Kindness Song

In 1994 Robie Lester Eccleston saw me being interviewed on a Los Angeles television program and was inspired to commit her own act of kindness. Robie decided to write a song about kindness, which is now our international theme song. It turns out that Robie is an ASCAP (American Society of Composers, Authors, and Publishers) writer and publisher.

If you, Dear Reader, are interested in the sheet music, please send us a self-addressed, stamped business-size envelope. Here is Robie's song.

A Random Act Of Kindness

If the world seems dark and gloomy,
I get out of bed and say
I can change the way it looks and see it
In a different way.

I can make the sun shine brightly
Even through a cloudy sky
And turn a tear
To a Thank You Dear
In the twinkling of an eye.

It's kind of a magic thing
But there's really nothing to it
Just make up your mind
That you'll be kind
And then go out and DO IT.

A Random Act of Kindness
Look around and you will see
That it's time you thought of the YOU YOU YOU
And forgot the me me me.

It can be very small
Or even as big as an ELEPHANT
So long as a Senseless Kindness is Committed
Then that's SWELL-A-PHANT.

A Random Act of Kindness
Doesn't cost a thing, it's free
It can make the world we live in,
A WONDERFUL PLACE A WONDERFUL PLACE
A WON-DER-FUL PLACE—TO BE!

Each One Of Us Makes A Difference

I t doesn't take a saint, professor or Nobel Peace Prize winner to positively influence the life of a youth. Anyone can give sound words of tolerance, nonviolence and love to strategically and creatively illustrate the importance of empowering one's self for the benefit of the community and the world. This is what I learned several months ago.

As a senior at the University of California at Santa Barbara (UCSB), nothing disturbed me more than my friends who believed that no one individual can make a real difference in the quality of our community, much less our world. Yet I knew that education and opportunity could unlock doors many never even knew existed, and I had to do something, but what?

The toughest part of accomplishing anything is getting the courage to start and to follow your aspirations. For me, this meant using my personal attributes to help inspire others for the sake of youth empowerment. The more I recognized the nobility and fulfillment of love and tolerance, the more passionate I became about empowering others with this information. It is education and opportunity that inspiration thrives on. Without them, apathy flourishes. Those who ignore or disregard the impact of those who have made a real difference, such as Dr. Martin Luther King, Nelson Mandela or even many of our own parents, pose the real challenge in the fight to overcome apathy and ignorance. I believe that love, awareness and empowerment are qualities that can never be trumped.

Diplomacy and knowledge of global affairs are extremely important in today's world, so I involved myself with many local experts on global issues who shared my objectives to help educate and empower our youth. Together we began to strategically organize a concrete, tangible approach to the problems my community faced. Santa Barbara needed a network of local organizations, university faculty and students to provide young people with information, opportunities and resources.

In January 2000 I pulled together the PAX 2100 International Forum, Nuclear Age Peace Foundation, United Nations Community Coalition, various UCSB departments and on-campus organizations to form this needed network for Santa Barbara youth. From its inception, the Global Studies Youth Initiative has outperformed my wildest expectations. With approximately thirty active members to date, we have educated much of the community about wide-ranging topics such as South American regimes and the United Nations. We were instrumental in adding a class on nonviolence to a local high school and educating students on the effects of foreign sweatshops. We have provided numerous internship opportunities for our partnering organizations, broken communication barriers between our partnering organizations (Amnesty International, Latin Business Association, Campus Labor Action Coalition) and the UCSB faculty, and we organized a summer trip to Mexico to work with El Centro de Immigrante to deliver medical supplies, construct houses, and feed the hungry.

Today, the Global Studies Youth Initiative provides education to Santa Barbara's youth on global issues, is a resource for humanitarian, political and environmental information, and is a place they can voice personal perspectives without unjust subjectivity.

At a recent UCSB Global Peace and Security reception, I received the first annual award for Outstanding Community Service and a $1,000 prize for my work. I am extremely honored and flattered by this recognition to help educate and empower youth in the community. It is my hope that others will realize that they too can make a real impact in people's lives.

~~Sean Fargo

Phone Call

Call a friend and tell her how much you miss her. Sometimes your friend can be lonely and may not have any family or other friends nearby to talk to. Call someone who is ill and brighten her day or offer to help her out if you can. Call someone who is elderly and visit with her for a few minutes on the phone.

Volunteering

You can volunteer your services to an individual or an organization that could use your help. There are a lot of people in need in this world. In the amount of time it takes to sit and think about the things we could do for others, we could already be out there doing them. Just get up and make a few calls and make that commitment.

Here are a few suggestions of places where you can volunteer:

- Offer help to a single parent
- Shop or run errands for someone elderly or ill
- Homeless shelters
- Animal shelters
- Hospitals
- Senior citizens homes
- Organizations for the mentally challenged
- Organizations for the physically challenged
- Schools
- Institutions for the blind
- Institutions for the deaf
- Libraries, teaching others to read
- Alliance for Family Violence

Selling Lemonade For Free

One day Katie and I were selling lemonade for 50 cents. The same day a lady was working so hard, we gave her a free cup, and she said, "Thank you very much!"

I said, "It was nothing." So from then on, we sold lemonade for free.

~~Danielle Curtis, 10 years old
Okinawa, Japan

This picture was illustrated by Catarina Gates, age 11.

Thank You, Mom

My mom, Carol Gates, is a single parent who works hard for her money so we can have food and shelter. She buys me clothes and also takes me to piano lessons.

I just wanted to say, "Thank you, Mom, for everything you have ever done for me." Her act of kindness is taking such good care of me. My act of kindness is to thank her for taking care of me.

Love,
Your daughter Catarina, age 11

Showing Appreciation

There are small things you can do to show appreciation to someone. A note or thank you card in the mail makes a tremendous impact to the person who committed a kind act. You can write a thank-you letter to family and friends letting them know how much they mean to you. It is a way for you to reflect on all the kind things that transpire in a family as well as a friendship. Where would you be without these wonderful people in your life to help encourage and support you? Is it worth picking up a pen and paper to find out?

Dear Joe,
  I really want to let you know how much your phone call meant to me last week. I am so glad to know that people still remember my son. Too often people don't want to talk about him in front of me because they think it will make me sad. They

New Year's Eve

O n December 31, 1997, I was traveling from
San Luis Obispo to Bakersfield. I had just
dropped off my son for a visit at my father's house.
Although the weather and traffic were no problem,
at about 4 p.m. my car stopped running. I was in a
hurry to pick up a curio cabinet for my home. I pushed
my car off the road onto the soft shoulder, and
checked under the hood to see what the problem
was. It was the serpentine belt—it was shredded all
over the engine and without one the car would not
run. I turned on my emergency flashers and left the
hood up hoping someone might stop. I stood by the
car watching traffic go by and got scared as daylight
slowly began to fade. It finally dawned on me that
this was New Year's Eve and soon everyone would
be out partying and there would be no one available
to help me. I was upset with myself that I had just
canceled my cell phone service because I just never
needed it.

Finally someone stopped to help. His name was
Bill and he worked for an electronic door company.
He allowed me to use his cell phone but, just as I
thought, no one was home. As tears streamed down
my face, Bill said he would take me to the nearest
town and informed me that he was headed to Oak
Liquidators in Bakersfield. Unbelievably, that was exactly where I was going to pick up my curio cabinet!
He took me to my home where thanks ensued. I asked
him to have the furniture store hold on to my curio
cabinet for me, and tell them I would pick it up as

soon as the car was repaired. I called the tow truck company to get my car and had to ride with him to pick it up. En route the driver was called about another woman stranded on the road. The driver said he would help her after he took care of my needs. I simply said, "Please don't leave her out there! Pick her up now and then take care of my car." We rescued the stranded woman, and eventually my car was towed home.

When my car was repaired, I went to pick up my cabinet from Oak Liquidators. They informed me that Bill told them all about what happened and that he asked them to hang on to the cabinet for me.

~~*Debbie Fogle*

What Goes Around Comes Around

I was standing in line to pay for my groceries in my local supermarket and noticed that the young girl in front of me was having trouble getting her ATM card to go through to pay for her items. The young woman had a baby just a few weeks old quietly lying in the carrier. This young mom kept lamenting to the cashier that she had just talked to the bank and there should not be any trouble with her ATM card. She started to panic and I could see tears welling up in her eyes as she pleaded, "Please keep trying. They said they had solved the problem."

Seeing that the young mother was very distressed, I looked to see what she was trying to purchase. She had formula, diapers, and some other very essential items she needed for her baby. I decided to hand my ATM card to the cashier and asked her to just charge me for the items. The young mother was noticeably upset and concerned about what she was going to do if she didn't leave with the things she needed for her baby. Still, she kindly said to me, "Oh, no, that's okay. I will figure this out."

I insisted that the cashier proceed to charge my card with the needed items, and the young girl thanked me very much. She asked for my address so she could mail me the money later. Denying her request, I told her that the only way I can repay an act of kindness that I have received is by helping in situations like hers. If she wouldn't allow me to commit my act of kindness, then I couldn't live up to my favorite saying: "What goes around comes around."

~~Joan Schraff

In about the same degree as you are helpful,
You will be happy.

~~Karl Reiland

The Snowstorm of 1999

During the thirty years I've lived in Bakers-field, California, I had never experienced a snowstorm. In fact, the 1999 snowstorm was the heaviest snow ever recorded here in at least a hundred years. The snow was beautiful, but it did lots of damage to the Magnolia trees in my front yard. I took my ordinary handsaw and went out to the front yard and began to clean up some of the mess. As I worked, a young boy about sixteen years old passed by, and we spoke casually as he went on his way. To my surprise, in about ten minutes he returned with a chain saw and said, "I came to help you."

Together we made tremendous progress in no time at all. Just before we were completely finished picking up all of the debris from the ground, the young man said that he hated to go with the job unfinished, but that he needed to leave right away. Before he left I went inside to get my billfold to pay him and he refused. He said, "I should pay you; it was a pleasure, and it was fun working with you." As I finished cleaning up what little was left, I watched him walk down to a house at the end of the street. Some time later I asked the gentlemen that lived in that house if that was his son who had helped me cut down the branches from my trees in my yard. The man said that it was his son, and that he had been at his house visiting. He went on to say that his son wasn't supposed to use the chain saw, but he felt so compelled to help me that he went against his father's wishes. I told the man he helped me out a lot. Not only did he "work like the dickens," but that he was pleasurable and very kind. I never did see the boy again, but his kind act has never been forgotten.

~~*Eileen Hatfield*

Doing The Unthinkable
The Language of Kindness

I own a small beauty salon, The Kindred Spirit, and it is located in the center of the large city where I live. I am learning new things about people all the time. As in any large city, there are people who live on the street in this area. I never knew that there was a difference in how people grew accustomed to living on the street but there is–almost as if it were a culture all of its own.

There are people who stand on the street corners asking for money or food, and there are those who quietly go about their own business providing for themselves by going through dumpsters and garbage bins. Some of those who ask for things can be quite brazen and rude at times and leave a bad impression in your mind about how other people living on the street may be.

Observing the rituals of some of these individuals, I have learned that the quieter ones look out for themselves and have such a sense of pride that they do not ask for or bother you about anything. These people aren't waiting for a handout. If you decide you would like to do something nice for one of them, you have to step out of your own comfort zone and enter that person's world. I found this quite interesting and sometimes difficult.

So now I have to do the unthinkable. I cook up a full course meal and take it to the garbage! I leave it beside the bin with a note attached for the "finder" to have a nice day or a Happy Holiday.

~~Joyce Otts

Abundant Help

I'll never forget how I felt when my stepfather, Edward Chaney, called me at work and told me that his best and oldest friend's son, Jason, had been murdered. Jason had just turned 18 and was only a week away from high school graduation. It was so overwhelming! I cried silently at my desk. My family had been going through some rough times financially, and we didn't have the money to pay our bills, much less enough money to buy a plane ticket to Seattle so Eddie could be there for his closest friend. It was tearing me up inside that there was nothing I could do for him or his friend, Sonny, or anyone else for that matter. As I was leaving work, I stopped in a co-worker's office to say goodbye. I was telling her how "stressed out" I was with everything that was going on.

My boss, Kris Johnson, overheard me and asked what was wrong. She took me into her office and I told her the story. She immediately said not to worry, that she would have the money to buy Eddie's plane ticket in my hand the next morning. She asked how much I needed. I was so shocked! After I booked the flight, I called my mother to tell her what had happened. It was a very emotional time for everyone. My mom and step-dad both cried. It was the nicest thing anyone has ever done for me! By the next day all of our family and friends had heard about what Kris had done.

The day Eddie was supposed to leave for Seattle, their phone was disconnected. That meant that we would have no way to communicate with Eddie while he was in Washington. He was so emotional. It broke our hearts to think we wouldn't be able to talk if he needed us, plus we were dealing with our own grief.

I think the kindness of Kris led to other amazing things. I was at work trying to figure out what to do about my mom and Eddie's phone when I received a phone call from my aunt, Patti Quijada. She told me that she called the phone company and paid their bill. The phone was turned back on that day! I called my mother right away. It startled her to hear the phone ring. I told her what Patty had done. Once again, there were more tears. I definitely believe that kindness is contagious. As Eddie was about to leave for the airport, we received a phone call from my grandmother, Gloria Bryant. Even though she didn't really have the money to give, she told Eddie that she would lend him some money for food and other necessities while he was traveling.

The three special people in this story have made a very big impact on my life and the lives of others. I can only hope that one day I will make such a profound difference in someone's life. Because of all they did for us, I try each and every day to commit at least one random act of kindness. Not only do I feel good about myself for doing it, I hope those I try to help feel good too, and that they will be more likely to pass on kindness and love to someone else.

~~*Karisa Talamantez*

Beyond Kindness

When Chuck Wall asked me to contribute to this new book on kindness, my first thought was to share some of the ways that I had performed a random act of kindness for someone else—for me what goes around comes around, and many times and in many ways over the years I have gone out of my way to assist another human being. But there was an act of kindness given to my family and me that impacted our family in a great way. I could never repay it except to do the work I do everyday on Power! Talk Radio. In 1996, when my life was on the rocks after a failed business venture, I had to leave my home in Chicago. Some incredible friends from upper Michigan arrived at my house, loaded our belongings into a horse trailer and headed back north with us in tow. In particular, Bruce and Pat Hardwick, owners of the Hillcrest Motel, housed my family for an entire year, rent free. We shared food and our faith and we became part of their family.

That act of kindness allowed me to reinvent my life and cocreate a radio show that touches thousands of lives everyday. This radio talk show was developed to help influence and bring positive ideas into the lives of others. Bruce and Pat are still my closest friends and we are up at that motel sitting around the table with major amounts of truth serum (coffee!) solving the challenges of the world at least three nights a week. One thing is for sure—without all the little things falling into place with the help of the Hardwicks and many others, Power! Talk Radio would not be on the airwaves. The ripple of kindness has no boundaries.

~~John St. Augustine
Radio Results Network
Newstalk 600 WCHT
Escanaba, Michigan
Power! Talk Radio

Adopt A Friend
The Language of Kindness

I work for a large cosmetic company and we deal with some of our customers for many years. One of the clients I received on the list to follow up on from my predecessor was a "mature" woman named Celeste. Celeste had been a customer with our company for many years. When she became ill with Parkinson's disease and was unable to pick up her products from the store, I offered to deliver the products to her and we soon became fast friends. She invited me over for lunch and to visit on many occasions. Because of my friendship with her, I have learned to have more patience with people shopping at our store and for the older customers in general. Celeste has enlightened me about the fact that people have a tendency to look right past her as if she were nonexistent, and that she just needs someone to converse with and be patient with her.

I am Hispanic and come from a large family that puts great value on the older members, and I assumed that all grandparents are treated as my own, but that is not always the case. This relationship makes me appreciate my own grandparents even more. Last year Celeste invited me to her Christmas dinner at the new retirement center she had just moved into. She could have chosen anyone to be her guest, but she selected me over all other family and friends. She said she appreciates my interest and concern in her and my phone calls and hugs. I don't do anything for Celeste because I feel sorry for her. I do it because I have affectionately adopted her, and I feel she is a member of my family now.

~~*Nicole Gonzales*

My Little Grandpa

I have a grandfather that I dearly love and enjoy. Unfortunately, I can't spend time with him since he lives in another state. He is the one person in my life who always had a calming, caring touch. If you stood next to him for even a moment, he would touch you either by putting his arm around you or, his favorite, scratching your back. You always knew he cared, not just because he had a contagious laugh and cute, funny remarks, but because of the warmth of his touch. No matter where I am or where I go, I can feel his gentle touch in my mind and hear that laugh in my head because it means something to me.

My grandmother was just as wonderful as my grandfather. Sadly, when she died of Alzheimer's disease, my dear grandfather became one of the lonely, elderly people not being touched in this world and with no one to touch, not because he isn't out there trying, but because no one has the time for him. This is a man who spent his whole life taking care of others, including raising my cousins.

Throughout my grandparents' lives they did for others, never getting that time alone they looked forward to in retirement. Sometimes it is too late in life to get the things we have waited for. Things don't happen the way we plan so we have to learn to enjoy and share each day of our life as it comes. I call my little grandpa and send cards but that isn't enough. I can't be there when he needs to have lunch or dinner with someone because he is lonely. I can only hope other family members will work him into their schedule. Sadly they usually can not, but perhaps you could. You can smile at him when you see him and give him a kind word, and you can know inside what he means to me. Maybe your loved one is the one I am being kind to in my area. I will continue to tell him that I love him; he needs to hear it and be reassured regularly because I can't show him the way that I would like to. He needs someone to be kind to him because he has shared great amounts of kindness with me and he would share his kindness with you too. Call someone you think might need a little reassurance today and tell him what he means to you. It doesn't matter who it is. Take the time to appreciate and acknowledge someone who may have no one.

~~Kimberly Walton

Gentle Reminder

I bought your bumper sticker that says, "Today, I will commit one random act of senseless KINDNESS... Will You?" and I put it on the rear window of my car. It is a gentle reminder to me to be a more patient and considerate driver. I can now allow other drivers to pull their cars over in front of me. This is my act of kindness. I have found that others who read my bumper sticker are more courteous to me too. Thank you for coming up with such a wonderful idea.

~~*Ms. Audrey M. Hack*

The Kindness Phrase
"Today, I will commit one random act of senseless KINDNESS... Will You?"

Chuck Wall coined the phrase above after hearing a radio announcer state, "Ladies and Gentlemen, I have another random act of senseless violence to report." From this Chuck developed a positive statement that became a classroom assignment. The phrase became known worldwide and is printed on bumper stickers, refrigerator magnets, T-shirts, posters and other products. It is designed to encourage positive thinking and challenge people to commit their own acts of kindness. By displaying this phrase on cars, trucks, office doors, bulletin boards or numerous other places that will be seen by others, you are supporting respect, dignity, compassion and humility—the four elements that define kindness.

The Universal Plot Theory

Accepting responsibility for our own personal behavior seems to be a major problem for many of us. Employers as well as teachers are constantly amazed at how creative employees and students become when making excuses for not being to work or school on time, or for not getting projects completed on schedule. Instead of admitting our own inability to manage time, we seek someone or something to blame for our own shortcomings. "I couldn't go to work on time because..." becomes a study in creativity that sometimes becomes quite humorous. The student who came to class late offered this excuse: "Sorry I'm late. I had car trouble."

"That's too bad," I said. "What was the problem with your car?" "My car couldn't find a parking place" came the prompt reply. Or the young woman who just didn't make it to class at all and was angry with me for marking her absent. "It's not my fault I wasn't there," she protested. "My car ran out of gas." The modern equivalent of "the dog ate my homework" is "my printer was out of ink, had a paper jam, didn't work today, plug was missing, etc." Employers often hear employees blame everyone except themselves.

"I'm late because my kids were slow getting ready; traffic was very heavy this morning; I couldn't find my keys; I got a phone call just as I was leaving the house; I had to stop for breakfast because I was running late and I know you don't want me to come to work hungry."

Excuses have become our justification for not doing what we committed ourselves to do at the time we said it would be done. Rarely do we hear, "I was late because I was totally unorganized this morning and obviously need to concentrate on developing time management skills." The Universal Plot Theory states that no matter what my problem is, it is caused by someone or something else. I cannot be held accountable for my behavior if the problem is not caused by me. Nations as well as political parties are no different than individuals. Excuses have become frequent diversion tactics to shift responsibility to someone else.

Each one of us must begin the difficult task of assessing our own involvement in the creation of the problems we lay at the feet of others. Analyzing our own behavior will begin the process of returning to basic personal responsibility for our own behavior rather than shifting the blame to others. Our courts are filled with law suits centering around plaintiffs who misused a product, violated a rule, broke a law or otherwise disregarded common sense and want to sue to justify their own lack of personal responsibility.

Let's all begin the process of returning respect and dignity to our own lives by accepting responsibility for our own actions. If we all engaged in this self-analysis, life would become significantly less complex and for more personally satisfying.

~~Chuck Wall, Ph.D.

Don't Ignore Nature's Kindness!

Early one morning when my friend Gord was sitting in his den, he heard a very pronounced rat-a-tat-tat, rat-a-tat-tat. Gord jumped up and went to check the propane stove. He thought the sound had come from there. He immediately shut off the gas and called the service man to come check everything out. When the repairman came, he said, "I get calls like this all the time. It's a woodpecker pecking on your pipe." However, as he continued to work, he discovered that there was a gas leak. What a potential for disaster this was! Everyone in the house was feeling pretty lucky as they walked the repairman to the door. They were very aware that this woodpecker's unwitting "act of kindness" might have saved their lives. They were glad they hadn't ignored nature's kindness.

"That was no bird—that was our angel of kindness!"

~~Linda Walton

A Cup Of Ice

The kids have orders not to touch the 17 cents sitting in the center console of Nigel Oliver's Chevy Blazer. Not that a kid can do much with 17 cents, but that's beside the point.

Those two nickels and seven pennies represent a man's gratitude, a man's pride. That pocket change signifies a stranger's stubborn reluctance to accept insult and defeat as part of some universal, irrevocable reality.

Nigel Oliver wants to hear those coins rattle around near his ashtray for a while longer. It'll remind him of a 101-degree day, a cup of ice and a walking, talking parable with a three-day beard.

It happened last week on a sweltering day in Bakersfield. It must have been around noon when a car pulled off the freeway south of Bakersfield and a short and wiry, 50-ish man with salt-and-pepper hair and a blue baseball cap, scrambled out from the passenger seat onto the dirt shoulder. He extracted his bags, which were attached to an aluminum luggage cart, and thanked the man who'd driven him up from Los Angeles.

Then he set out for town. It was a long, miserable trudge up Union Avenue, and by the time he reached a bustling roadside mini-market, he must have been about ready to evaporate in his work boots.

He staggered into the convenience store, filled his insulated, 32-ounce coffee cup from the ice machine and stepped to the back of the line. When he reached the front, the clerk looked him over. "Eighty-nine cents," he said.

The salt-and-pepper man didn't need to rummage through his pockets. He hadn't expected a cup of ice to cost quite so much, and he knew he didn't have it. Realizing this, the clerk took the man's cup, walked over to a sink and poured the ice down the drain.

Perhaps accustomed to such humiliations, the salt-and-pepper-haired man walked back out through the double-glass doors and calmly sat down on a curb. He took out an old, mottled rag and wiped off his sweaty arms and forehead.

That's what he was doing when Oliver, who'd stopped there to gas up his '85 SUV, found him. Oliver had watched the whole thing unfold inside the store, and after he'd paid for his gas and his Gatorade, he walked over to the man.

Did he need anything? A Coke?

No thanks.

A beer? The man hadn't had a drink in 11 years, and he wasn't about to start again now. In fact, the stranger said, he was just fine. Oliver went back into the store anyway and filled his own 64-ounce plastic mug with ice. After some prodding, the man accepted it.

Oliver asked him his name. "Charles," the man answered, "but friends call me Charley. You," Charley said, "can call me Charley."

Oliver asked him where he was headed. Charley wasn't sure. "Probably into town," he said. Oliver told him he could get a meal and a break from the heat at the Bakersfield Homeless Center.

Could he use a little bus fare to get himself there? "No thanks," Charley responded. He could walk.

"You'll fry first," Oliver said. "It's a mighty long walk, and today's a mighty hot day."

Charley thought this over for a minute. He said he had a couple of dollars in food stamps he could pay in exchange for a ride. "Hop in," said Oliver, "but don't worry about the food stamps." Oliver tossed in Charley's luggage cart with its small suitcase, backpack and shaving kit, and they drove away.

It was only after he'd delivered his passenger to the Bethany Center and then driven a few blocks toward home that Oliver noticed the coins resting on the little tray of his vehicle's center console —17 cents that hadn't been there before. Seventeen cents that might have represented all the money Charley had at the time.

When he talks about the incident now, Oliver is alternately sad and irate. He thinks about the cup of ice that went down the drain and how much good it might have done.

"How can you deny a man a cup of ice?" asks Oliver, who works overnight shifts as a pumper for a Kern County oil refinery. "In the city that started the Random Acts of Kindness thing, that's pretty bad."

There's more than one irony at work here though. The mini-market chain that turned away the overheated stranger is a regular contributor to at least one homeless program in Bakersfield. It's the sort of program that takes homeless and destitute people, vagrants, hobos, mentally ill, whatever they might be, out of settings like the one at the convenience store and places them in environments where they can get help.

The idea is to pass out confidence along with corned-beef hash, and self-esteem along with blankets and pillows. If a homeless man walks out into the world each morning with a full belly, good. If he walks out with more pride in himself, with a greater resolve than when he checked in, even better.

It's that very principle, though, that gives Nigel Oliver pause when he reflects on Charley and his 17 cents. Charley, he believes, already possesses a healthy measure of pride and resolve. He's got some self-esteem, some integrity, some dignity. All he wanted was a cup of ice.

~~*Robert Price*
The Bakersfield Californian
August 6, 2000

This Old Friend

About 12 years ago my father lost a long battle with breast cancer (something not common in men). Even though you know the end is coming, it is still a shock to you when the actual time occurs.

Through this ordeal I had an old friend that did just what I needed at the time; he listened. I would go over to his house and sit with him, or work with him on a project and he would listen as I rambled on. He seemed to sense the pain I was going through. He never tired of my talking, never passed judgment and would tell me it was O.K. to feel the way I did. Every time we would get together, he seemed to know how to keep my mind busy. Every time I came away from him, I would feel a little better and less empty. I don't think I ever thanked him for all he did for me at that time in my life.

The reason I'm writing this story is to tell this old friend of mine thank you for all he did for me when I was grieving over my father's death. This old friend of mine is Chuck Wall. You truly did do an act of kindness with your patience and listening. I truly want to thank you for that now. Thank you!

~~*Craiger Bolen*

The Birds

When I had a heart attack and was sent to the hospital for open-heart surgery, I was very concerned about my birds (2 cockatiels, 4 canaries, and 1 finch) and about my dog Tu Shu who is my 15-year-old companion. My next-door neighbor was among the many who visited me in the hospital and she offered to take care of my birds for me. Bless her heart, I don't think she knew what she was getting into. It took three long months before I could get back home. She had a great amount of help from her three daughters and her husband. Believe me, it helped in my recovery to know my birds were being well taken care of. I'm so grateful to this kind neighbor who still helps me by shoveling snow and doing numerous other things for me. It's neighbors like mine that prove that kindness is alive and well in my neighborhood.

~~*Rosemary S. Landrucker,*
Fort Wright, Kentucky

Mary, My Rock

My postal worker Mary Breeding delivers more than mail to people in need. She delivers friendship, kindness and help. She has been on my mail route for years, but we started visiting one day after her brother died from AIDS. When she found out that I was dealing with a disease called lupus and fibromyalgia, she began to do things to help me out. She said that in the late stages of her brother's disease she found out what a difference it made in the quality of his life to be given the gift of time from caring volunteers. So she lives her life giving to others whenever she can.

Mary works full time and has her own family to care for, but she always finds time to help me when I need it. When I had a cardiac arrest, she was one of the first ones to visit me at the hospital, and during my weeks of confinement to bed, she did all my grocery shopping, picked up my medications, and even walked my dog after she got off work. She would take my laundry home with her and did anything she could to make me comfortable. Gabrielle, Mary's twelve-year-old daughter, told her one day, "I hope when I grow up that I can find a nice lady to help like you help Pat." Her friendship and caring has meant the difference between me going into a board-care facility or staying in my own home. I am very thankful for this wonderful person as well as her family, and Mary will always be "my rock."

~~Pat Palmgren

An Angel?

My story begins about two years ago. My grandfather had become quite ill and was rapidly decreasing in health with Alzheimer's disease. The time had arrived; my grandmother could no longer care for her love as she had been. His health had deteriorated and he decided that he was ready to die. The doctor had him put into a full-care facility where he could be monitored.

The staff couldn't get him to do anything and he had given up. He wouldn't eat and would throw his food at them and tell them to leave. He was miserable and unsure of his surroundings.

We were told a nurse from the independent living side came walking through one day offering her assistance, and because of her resemblance to me, my grandfather allowed her to help.

She was the only one besides family that he would let come near him without feelings of anger and aggression. She didn't have to help my grandfather but she did. We heard that she was very kind, even though we never met her, and I believe that she worked the night shift. A few weeks after my grandfather passed away my grandmother went to take something special to the wonderful nurse that helped out my grandfather so much. Because no one knew her name and the staff found no one fitting her description that worked on the independent living side, this wonderful person remains a mystery to us.

My grandmother will always believe this was an angel and she might be right. However, maybe it's possible that it was someone visiting the facility that realized she could help my grandfather when others could not. She continued to make her helpful visits until my grandfather's death.

Was she an angel? We will never know, but what we do know is that her kindness added life to my grandfather. Thank you mystery person—angel.

~~*Lisa Brunelle*

Salome and Ophelia
The Language of Kindness

I grew up in Namibia, with my mother who was very prejudiced, as were many people. During the time that I lived in Johannesburg, South Africa (1976/77), I worked at a civil engineering company. Salome, the elderly black lady who collected and delivered the company mail to the post office, cleaned the office, and made tea and coffee for the staff, was a very gentle and kind person. After we got to know each other better, I asked her if she knew of anyone who would be interested in doing laundry and ironing for me. She recommended one of her daughters, Ophelia. Salome had several children ranging from adults to primary school age.

Ophelia came to work for me and did a great job; I referred her to several of my friends, who were also very pleased with her performance and dependability. This was during the rioting in Soweto, the black township, outside of Johannesburg. During this period of rioting Salome came to work very perplexed. I asked her what was the matter and she told me that she had warned her younger children to stay home from school and lock themselves inside the house, not to go out for any reason at all, even if she did not make it back home that night. Ophelia was also in town that day. By the end of the day Salome confided in me that she was very concerned about going to Soweto that night because she knew there was going to be a major riot. But where was she going to stay? She could not afford to stay in a hotel; besides there were not that many hotels in the city where black people could stay because of apartheid. I could tell she was really afraid.

Ophelia had joined her after work. After chatting with them for a while, I decided to take them to my apartment and have them spend the night with me. In South Africa at that time this was not just a matter of friends staying over or helping someone out. During apartheid it was against the law to have black people stay with whites unless you had detached "quarters" for them. Many houses had this type of accommodation because they had live-in maids and men servants. This was a very scary thing to do. I had to sneak them into the apartment complex, hopefully undetected, as black people had to have passes and they were not to be seen on the streets at night. We had dinner together and talked a little, but everyone was very nervous. Thankfully it was not as bad getting them out the next morning. Since it was daytime, it was common to see black people in the building. This experience brought us all closer together and we realized that there really wasn't any difference between us except the color of our skins. It especially affected how I felt towards black people because I grew up in a home filled with prejudice.

I left South Africa later in 1977 and traveled through Europe, ending up in America. I started an import business in 1984 bringing in crafts and fine art from South Africa. I believe my experience helping Salome and Ophelia allowed me to better assist other black people in South Africa to develop products by using skills they already had and working with other white South Africans, who also wanted to treat the black people fairly and help them to get ahead. Since then I have worked with many black people and was invited to stay in their homes during my business trips. In the new South Africa whites and blacks are living together in the same neighborhoods.

My experiences in South Africa have proven to me that people around the world, regardless of skin color or language, want the same things in life. That is a safe environment to live in, love in their family, independence, and pride in their achievements. Kindness is universal and should always be a part of our daily lives.

~~Olga See

The entire sum of existence is the magic of being needed by just one person.

~~Vi Putman

The Carousel Horse
A Pass-along Thank You

In December 1996 my husband Eddy and I flew from our home in Bakersfield, California, to Oklahoma City, Oklahoma, to visit relatives.

While we were on a Christmas shopping trip, we drove through the small town of Yukon. As we went by the downtown stores, I spotted the most beautifully decorated carousel horse in the window of an antique shop. Since it was a Sunday, the store was closed so we decided to return the next day. The carousel horse was even more beautiful up close. I fell in love with it and decided I had to have it. The clerk assured me she could have it shipped to my house. So I paid for it, and paid an extra amount for the shipping. Thinking all was well, we flew home the following day.

After about a week the clerk from the store called with bad news. She couldn't find anyone to ship the horse to our home because at a height of four feet it was too big for either UPS or parcel post, and too expensive for a moving van or for airfreight. The clerk said she was sorry and she would mail our check back.

On the same day we received our returned check, the clerk from Oklahoma called again to ask if we still wanted the horse. The helpful clerk had solved our problem. A couple who came into the store happened to mention they were traveling to Bakersfield for the holidays to be with relatives. After hearing our story, they said they would be happy to deliver our horse to us.

Late in the afternoon on December 22 those wonderful people arrived at our door with my beautiful carousel horse. I happily thanked them for their large delivery of kindness.

Star Royeton

INDEX OF STORIES

103D CONGRESS
2D SESSION
H. RES.____

IN THE HOUSE OF REPRESENTATIVES

Mr. Tucker submitted the following resolution, which was referred to the Committee on
February 8, 1994

RESOLUTION

𝕰xpressing the sense of the House of Representatives that the people of the United States should be encouraged to practice random acts of kindness.

𝖂hereas the incidence of random acts of violence in the United States has reached epidemic levels;

𝖂hereas the Surgeon General of the United States estimates that, every day in the United States, 135,000 children carry guns to school;

𝖂hereas, every day in the United States, 3 children are killed by child abuse, 9 children are murdered, 13 children are killed by guns, 30 children are wounded by guns, 307 children are arrested for crimes of violence, 7,945 children are reported abused or neglected, and 5,703 teenagers are victims of violent crime;

𝖂hereas every 4 hours a child in the United States commits suicide;

𝖂hereas, in the United States, every 6 minutes a rape is committed, and every year between 3,000,000

and 4,000,000 women are battered by their part-
ners and more than 200,000 women are stalked;

Whereas, every year in the United States, there are
4.7 random acts of violence committed against
every 1,000 persons 65 years of age or older;

Whereas, every year in the United States, there are
758.1 random acts of violence for every 100,000
persons in the United States, and 235 firearm-
related acts of violence for every 100,000 persons in the United States;

Whereas, there are 238,000,000 handguns in the
United States;

Whereas, in 1992 in the United States, there were
1,730 anti-Semitic incidents, the total number
of white-supremacist groups rose 27 percent
above the number from the previous year, and a
record number of bias-related incidents, including 31 murders, were reported;

Whereas hate crimes against Asians comprised 8.9
percent of all hate crimes documented in Los
Angeles County in 1990;

Whereas the United States strongly opposes random
acts of violence, and all forms of intolerance and
mean-spiritedness based on ethnicity, religion,
race, gender, or sexual orientation; and

Whereas Dr. Charles Wall of Bakersfield Community
College has committed his efforts to promoting
random acts of kindness among all people: Now,
therefore, be it

Resolved, That it is the sense of the House of Representatives that the people of the United States
should be encouraged to practice random acts
of kindness, in the spirit of compassion, kindness, and goodwill toward all persons.

There is no end to this book...
...just pass along the Kindness.

Kindness Bill

Bill To: _____

The act of kindness that I have committed comes with a price. This price is difficult for some to pay, but it is customary where an act of kindness is concerned. I hope not to inconvenience you too much, but this is all I ask of you.

The price that I want is for you to allow me to commit my act of kindness free of charge. If you allow me to present this act of kindness to you, then I will receive the joy I would like to receive for committing it.

Your portion of the bill is paid in full when you truly enjoy the act itself, without feeling as though you owe me something in return. The fulfillment I get from this is all I want. So consider your bill paid in full!